WHERE WILL I DO MY
PINEAPPLES?

The little book of building
a whole new school

Gill Kelly Edited by Ian Gilbert

Crown House Publishing Limited
www.crownhouse.co.uk - www.crownhousepublishing.com

First published by

Crown House Publishing Ltd
Crown Buildings, Bancyfelin, Carmarthen, Wales, SA33 5ND, UK
www.crownhouse.co.uk

and

Crown House Publishing Company LLC
6 Trowbridge Drive, Suite 5, Bethel, CT 06801, USA
www.crownhousepublishing.com

First published 2011.

British Library Cataloguing-in-Publication Data
A catalogue entry for this book is available
from the British Library.

Print ISBN 978-184590696-2

Kindle ISBN 978-184590761-7
ePub ISBN 978-184590762-4

LCCN 2011925282

Printed and bound in the UK by
Gomer Press, Llandysul, Ceredigion

To Alan, without whom,
I would not have got this far

Foreword

The first time I entered a new school funded by the Labour government's ambitious Building Schools for the Future (BSF) scheme I was amazed. It was the most striking school building I had ever seen at a time when many schools were either Victorian factory-model buildings with high windows and an intractable sense of oppression or else 1960's boxes with the smell of hopelessness growing as virulently as the moss on the leaking flat roofs of the mobile classrooms.

This school was different though. Gleaming, spacious, full of light, a great sweeping ark of a building that proclaimed loudly that learning was important, that children counted, that truly the very physical fabric of this thing called a 'school' had entered the twenty-first century.

'The architect designed it so that the classrooms could be flexible but the teachers just rearranged everything to sit the students in rows facing the front,' said my host for the visit.

I was gobsmacked.

Here was an opportunity on a very shiny award-winning plate to transform the nature of teaching and learning for the better and staff had recreated the old model in the skin of the new one. It was at this point that I realised the extent to which the BSF scheme was going to fail in so many cases, that the government was going to waste its money as the schools wasted their opportunities. It was on that afternoon that I realised that the whole multimillion pound project called BSF was in trouble and the phrase BSF:SOS was born – BSF: Same Old Shit.

But let me take you back to the turn of the eighteenth century and a Geography teacher from Scotland named James Pillans. He was credited with the idea of taking the slates that the children were using to write down their learning and putting them together on the wall. This, according to one particular view of history, is how the blackboard was born.

By writing in chalk the teacher was now able to put the knowledge stored in his or her head out there for all learners to see. And the seeing was important. With something to look at it now made sense to arrange the room in such a way that the learners could see, especially with mixed-aged classes, with the bigger children at the back, the smaller ones at the front and the teacher somewhere between the two depending on whether they were expounding or monitoring. The 'gallery' classroom model, developed by Samuel Wilderspin (who also invented the idea of the playground) supported the didactic model of teaching with the children as passive recipients of the teacher's knowledge, putting questions to the teacher and answering questions posed by the teacher, all with the help of the new-fangled chalkboard.

Apart from the fact that the teacher doesn't need to write anything these days and the information can be in video form, the interactive whiteboard is the direct descendent of Pillans's invention and, although it can be used to go way beyond just being a twenty-first century black, green or white board, often it just isn't.

The architecture of the classroom matched perfectly the paradigm of the teaching and learning and then very little changed, in either, for a hundred years or so and, as with the shining BSF school I visited, even when it could change, it didn't.

Which is why we were delighted to be approached by Gill Kelly when she was at Nailsea to help her in the school's project to use the new building as a lever by which she could try to create a new style of teaching and learning, to create a new paradigm that, if not doing away with the old one, would at least offer an element of choice and variety when it came to choosing what worked best.

And cancelling the multi-thousand pound order for interactive whiteboards in every classroom and encouraging them to move away from James Pillans's model as the *only* way classrooms could look was the starting point.

This potential to make bold decisions was backed up by the research which underlined the tremendous opportunity that the BSF programme was giving schools:

There is no specific agreed definition of what constitutes educational transformation. However, schools going through the process have a clear understanding of the areas most important to them for assessing the extent to which BSF delivers educational transformation. This includes more personalised teaching and learning and improving the life chances of children into their adult lives. Headteachers are confident that BSF can contribute to raising standards in school and beyond, by extending the benefits of their facilities to the wider community. In the case of the former, there was a recognised need to build capacity of staff to enable them to deliver a personalised teaching and learning experience to their pupils, though our research has indicated that schools, in particular, need a greater level of clarity on what educational transformation is.

(DCSF, 2010)

How many schools actually followed though on this opportunity and changed things fundamentally – or at least tried to change things like Gill Kelly and the other members of the team at Nailsea – is, I believe, a different thing altogether.

Of course, since those heady days when new schools cropped up like mushrooms, the current government has cancelled the future and its review into BSF talks of waste, inefficiency and costs out of control. We may never see such an ambitious programme again.

Because of that, what Gill has captured in this book, is a valuable once-in-a-lifetime insight into one ordinary school's extraordinary approach to significant change that, while based around a BSF project, is actually relevant in any change management process. The way the school went about being brave, asking big questions, expecting answers from partners who would rather pull the wool over their eyes and sell them 'kit' that didn't add any value to learning, the way they engaged the whole staff, the way they worked with hearts and minds and the way they followed through on their ambitions and made sure that their vision became as much of a reality as it possibly could – all of this means there is a great deal to be learned from what one school did in a sleepy backwater in the south-west of England.

Wherever there is change, significant change, there is significant opportunity. This is what this book is about. And where there is change, of course, there will be questions about pineapples ...

Ian Gilbert
France
July 2011

Acknowledgements

If I am living proof that having significant, supportive adults in your childhood creates successful confident people, then I have to acknowledge the part my parents played in this. Through their unwavering love and belief in my abilities, I have achieved more than I thought possible.

I would like to acknowledge my indebtedness to the Independent Thinking 'family' of associates who have supported me in many ways throughout the journey, especially Jim Smith who acted as the main funnel between what the school needed and what Independent Thinking could offer. And, of course, my thanks and appreciation goes to all my colleagues at Nailsea School, especially David New, the head teacher.

I would also like to thank David New and Peter Scholey for permission to use 'A Beautiful School' in Appendix 1 and Trudy Jones and David New for permission to use 'A Day in the Life of a Year 8 Student (2010)', in Appendix 2.

Contents

Foreword vii

Acknowledgements xiii

Introduction: Don't Let the Bean Counters Take Over! .. 1

1. I'm the Tena Lady 9

2. Science Isn't a Subject, It's a Philosophy 23

3. Forming Relationships and Engendering
   Commitment 37

4. Conventional Toilets, Standard Classrooms 49

5. I Think It Went OK but Not Really Good 59

6. No, Really, Where Will I Do My Pineapples? 77

Appendix 1: A Beautiful School 93

Appendix 2: A Day in the Life of a Year 8 Student (2010) .. 99

Appendix 3: Summary of Building Schools for the
            Future ICT Consultation Sessions 103

Appendix 4: CPD Learning Loop 109

Appendix 5: Curriculum Design: Our Starting Point
            (September 2008) 113

Appendix 6: What If... ? by Ian Gilbert 123

Bibliography 133

Introduction: Don't Let the Bean Counters Take Over!

When I heard the news, I literally let out a scream of joy and hugged the nearest person. This happened to be the other deputy head, Steve Richards, but if it had been anyone else I would have done just the same.

Nailsea School had just been given the news that we had been allocated £32 million as part of the government's Building Schools for the Future (BSF) programme to rebuild our age-ing 1959 school. But don't get me wrong. It wasn't just about the money. For too long the buildings of this large secondary school in the south-west had dictated the teaching that went on in the classrooms, often with scant regard for the learning. The campus was made up of 'boxes' of a uniform nature of the sort you may well see if you are a teacher reading this at school and look out of your window. There was a regulation assembly hall, sports hall, school playing field and everything else you would expect from a late 1950's school. As a result, a nineteenth century, broadly didactic form of pedagogy pre-vailed.

But now the school was being given the chance to transform learning, and we were going to grab it with both hands.

So began the three-year process that led to us moving into our shiny new building in September 2009; three years of hard work that resulted in a resounding success story in terms of academic achievement and community building and a rapturous response from staff, students and parents. What was our secret? In a nutshell, we had been radical in our vision, firm in demanding adherence to our moral purpose and quick on our feet when it came to problem solving.

Easy to say now, but a great deal harder to achieve when you are in the thick of it and the clock is ticking.

It is all too common, when faced with a build project, for schools to focus on details like the number of rooms needed, the length of cable required for ICT and the best furniture for the school canteen – and to do all of this *before* you have even considered the nature of learning and how it can be enhanced by a new environment and the technology in it.

Too many schools are still making this mistake. When we began our project in September 2006, Nailsea was in the second wave of the BSF roll-out. However, although we saw sparkling new schools in beautifully landscaped surroundings from the first wave, we did not witness a radical approach to learning being promoted through the build programme.

My challenge, as part of a team, was to transform learning and, as far as I was concerned, I would not settle for anything less. This required a great deal of input from all the key stakeholders – governors, teachers, students, parents, the education authority and, importantly, the leaders of the wider community. However, this was to be not a school designed by committee, but one that took the views of a wide range of people, turned them into a vision and used that as the backbone for the entire project.

If I had to identify one element that was the key to the success of the project – from the design and erection of the new building to the choice and installation of the ICT equipment – it was this: keep the human element uppermost in all discussions and at all times. This is very easy to lose sight of when you are discussing how many RJ45 sockets you want in the school and the perceived merits of either Cat 5 or Cat 6 cabling. Which is where I came in.

As deputy head in charge of curriculum and standards my role during the build project was not only to contribute to the design stages but also, more importantly, to represent the school's vision for learning, especially in the ICT contract element of the project. As a self-confessed 'non-techie', this was no mean feat. Entering the world of ICT was a bit like being parachuted into a foreign country in the middle of a civil war, in the dark, with no torch, no map and no ability to speak the language. In fact, one of the very first things I had to do was to find an 'interpreter' who could translate the technospeak. Only then could I actually start the job of designing the school.

This book is a result of my sink-or-swim experience – an opportunity to share what I learned with colleagues who find themselves in a similar situation, in the hope that I can help you to avoid some of the mistakes we made, as well as enabling you to take on board our successes and adapt these for your own school.

It is aimed primarily at senior leaders engaged in a rebuild or refurbishment programme and focuses on a range of strategic issues that you will need to get right, each one followed by a checklist of do's and don'ts. Think of it as a guidebook for your own voyage of discovery where, apart from finding out about the nature of a complex build programme with multiple funding streams and 'competitive dialogues', you will also discover much about yourself, what you stand for and what kind of leader you are.

You will be challenged to think differently and you will need to encourage others to think differently too; you must take these people with you (or nearly all of them) on their own journey to make what is on paper and in your heads become a reality. In fact, if you get to the end of a three-year educational build programme and you have not challenged yourself in these areas, then you will have failed.

In the same way that a building needs a foundation, a change process needs a structure and the one that worked well for us was the stages of human evolution designed by psychologist Clare W. Graves, which was taken up by Christopher Cowan and Don Beck in their book *Spiral Dynamics*.

Clare W. Graves was a psychologist working in the US from the 1940s through to the 1970s and is the creator of the spiral dynamics model. He wanted to provide a clear system that explained the ever-shifting nature of human development. Spiral dynamics shows how the mature adult brain can exist on any of eight spirals of evolution and how each stage of evolution is dependent upon another. During our journey towards a new school, this approach to looking at the psychological structure of human beings and the way they work proved to be incredibly useful.

The table overleaf is to be read from left to right, starting with someone's world view, through to their level of existence and corresponding behaviours. So, if you have no world view (like a newborn child) you are in survival existence, and your behaviours will focus on eating, sleeping and sexual behaviours for reproduction (if an adult).

Similarly, if your view is that the world is in chaos, you will be in the existence of order and your behaviours would focus on achieving strong structures and hierarchies to take control.

For more information on spiral dynamics visit www.clarewgraves.com.

World Views, Levels of Human Existence and Corresponding Behaviours

World View	Eight Levels of Human Existence	Thinking/Behaviour
All things are dependent on each other for survival	Interdependent	Global, holistic
The world is complex	Interconnected	Systems thinking
We are all equal	Community	Empathy, collaboration
Full of opportunities	Enterprise	Working for personal reward in the medium and long term
The world is in chaos	Order	Hierarchy, rules, structure
Only the strong survive	Self	Impulsive, power, instant gain
Unsafe, mysterious, strange forces around us	Tribal	Family, icons, rituals
No world view at this level	Survival	Eat, sleep, sex

This book was written at a very interesting time in the UK, both economically and politically. In May 2010, Gordon Brown's Labour Government was voted out of power to be replaced by a Conservative/Liberal Democrat Coalition Government led by David Cameron. The Coalition has promised not only to solve the deficit in the economy but also to transform our education system. Not long after the election, the Secretary of State for Education, Michael Gove, announced the cancellation of the Building Schools for the Future programme – with 700 schools having their projects terminated. In its place we are seeing the introduction of technical academies and free schools. Where this will take us no one knows.

I am also writing this as I prepare myself for my new role as principal of the City Academy Bristol. As it was the first academy to be built in the south-west, I will be perfectly placed to observe the impact of a new build not only on educational standards, but also on the wider community. I am proud to be taking over not only an innovative school building, but a community that has had its aspirations raised both as a result of capital input and the way in which the build programme was used to innovate.

Results at the City Academy Bristol have risen year on year, and the facilities it can boast about have become a true community resource. The school is open 363 days a year, and sports facilities are let on a continual basis, as well as being a base for one of the city's football clubs, Bristol City. It is a good example of how putting learning first in a build programme can have far reaching effects.

So, take from this book what you need, take it with you on your journey of discovery and, before you embark, ensure that your moral compass is set to true north.

Good luck and enjoy the ride!

Chapter 1

I'm the Tena Lady

There are three constants in life ... change, choice and principles.

Stephen Covey

One of my strong memories of the 'visioning conference' in the first year of our build programme was of a teaching colleague delivering a presentation on school design to 300 people. The audience was made up of staff, students, governors, local authority representatives, government officials and eminent delegates from the world of architecture.

The focus of the talk was the layout of the 'learning space' (a classroom in old money), with particular reference to the proximity of toilets. To describe this particular colleague as eccentric would be a bit of an understatement, but she ended the presentation with a plea to the listening throng to consider the plight of young people with bladder weaknesses. As she sat down from her exposition she whispered in my ear the immortal words, 'I'm the

9

Tena Lady.'* As a senior leader I failed miserably to keep it together after that and I giggled throughout the next two presentations.

My point is that my wonderful colleague was concerned about the details of a learning institution and how they would affect the people within it. The staff and students of the new school environment had survival needs that had to be met. However, before we could consider such tiny – but significant – details, we had to dig deeper still and get to the root of our moral purpose. We had to answer three important questions:

1. Why are we here?

2. What as educationalists do we want to get out of this process?

3. How will we approach the responsibility of building learning for the future?

The conference, which was conceived by the school's head teacher, David New, was intended to stretch the thinking of the delegates – to get them to consider alternatives to the nineteenth-century model of teaching and to capture the opinions of stakeholders on the future of education. In particular, we wanted their views on how a learning school should look in the twenty-first century.

To achieve this we had to examine our moral purpose as educators and create a vision from there. What evolved from the conference became for us a seminal document,

---

* Tena produce a range of products for people with bladder problems.

'A Beautiful School' (see Appendix 1), which became the guiding force for the project and gave us the strength to resist outside pressure to do things 'their way'. This was soon joined by another hugely important document, 'A Day in the Life of a Year 8 Student' (see Appendix 2), which also visualised what we were hoping for at the completion of the project.

Will Ryan in his book *Leadership with a Moral Purpose* comments on the pressures faced by schools and the responsibility we have as leaders to hijack the agenda in the interests of children and their learning:

In short the pressures all come from the outside into the school. The time has come to turn the processes inside out. Those who have the knowledge and understanding of a school and its community should claim autonomy and turn primary education inside out. They should lead the school to a brighter and better future through their own minds, hearts and knowledge of the community they are serving. They should use the best of the outside – without being a government puppet. The balance of power needs to shift towards those who have the expertise, the passion, the energy, and the belief to do the right thing. (Ryan, 2008: ix)

It is important to remember that architects, quantity surveyors, local authority project managers and the like are *not* educators. You will be confronted with BB98 (a briefing framework for secondary school projects) and many other restrictive formulae for your project. Remember, this is not legislation; it is *guidance*. There will be many voices telling you what you can't do. Hold your nerve. You are the lead professional in terms of education. It is vital that you challenge what you are told and justify all decisions from an educational perspective. This is particularly true when it comes to ICT. Do not be fobbed off with technospeak or seduced by 'kit', terabytes or megahertz. In fact, when it comes to ICT have just one golden rule: if it doesn't have a positive impact on learning, don't bother.

It is also important to remember who you are doing this for: your current students and the thousands of students who will follow them deserve the very best learning environment which reflects the value of an excellent education. Even though there will be many more reasons to play safe than to be adventurous, resist them. Be courageous. Do not let the children down.

To be a brave leader, I had to be sure of our ground when it came to our vision for learning. To achieve this, the school embarked on a journey of exploration and analysis to come up with the answer to the question 'What is learning?' This is where Ian Gilbert, founder of Independent Thinking, came into the picture. It was October 2007, and Ian had come to deliver an INSET day. He had the staff roaring with laughter and thinking differently at the same time. He really challenged them to look at education in a different way.

Ian gave me the idea of putting together a 'Learning Manifesto' – a declaration of belief for the way we wanted learning to be in our school. I began the process of consulting with staff, students and parents, something that was very painful at times, as it made them challenge the status quo – something many people had invested time and energy into keeping over the years, but the outcome was the Nailsea School Learning Manifesto which established the backbone for our 'language of learning'.

Nailsea School Learning Manifesto

We believe that:

1. Nailsea School is an inspirational learning community, where every member is regarded as a learner.

2. Learning does not happen in a vacuum; a positive emotional sense of well-being is vital in the learning process.

3. There are differences in the ways boys and girls learn.

4. All staff have a role to play in fostering a desire to learn as well as encouraging ambition, hope and optimism in our learners.

5. Lesson design is based on the concept of 'high challenge, low stress' and will stretch the abilities of all learners without anxiety or pressure.

6. It is acceptable for people to make mistakes and fail and be rewarded for trying.

7. The learning brain is one which requires stimulation, oxygen, water, movement and review in order to make connections between brain cells.

---

8. Learning is not about 'one size fits all'; learners have multiple intelligences and achieve in different ways.

9. Learners are responsible for their learning and should be involved in the development of learning strategies.

10. Learning should be real and make connections with the world we live in.

11. A common language to facilitate learning should be used within the school as well across phases.

The vocabulary was important as we needed an agreed way of talking about teaching and learning. As a school community, we had to establish the shared understanding of how effective learning was going to be achieved otherwise we would be creating a new campus that would be simply a great thrill or a huge disappointment, depending on your outlook on education. I am not saying that we managed to get all staff signed up to the Learning Manifesto, but it made the expectations of the school very clear and its values were woven into our lesson observation criteria.

My point is that without a shared understanding of what learning is, and why we as professionals get out of bed each day, it will not be possible to create a vision for a school that is *owned* by the community it serves. The Learning Manifesto may well be similar to something you already have in your school, or it may not, but the *process* of creating the document led the contributors to examine what they stood for and why they were there. As an institution, we then had to establish a commitment to that view of learning that would be evident in every brick and every pane of glass in the new school.

Now, that is a big step! But we did it.

The other main component was to set to work on our vision for the ICT. An important point to bear in mind is never start with what kinds of technology you want in your new school. Focus instead on what would aid effective learning and *then* ask how the kit can enable this to happen.

If you have built castles in the air, your work need not be lost; that is where they should be. Now put foundations under them.

Henry David Thoreau

To be frank, you don't find many philosophers in the world of ICT; at least you don't at local authority level or within schools. I find this situation perplexing as technology has the power to truly transform learning – if it is deployed well. However, if set up badly it slows down learning, frustrates staff and can waste inordinate amounts of money that could be better used elsewhere. It was absolutely vital, therefore, that the learning castle we built in the air had some seriously solid foundations, fully supported by cutting-edge technology.

So we embarked on an ICT visioning process with staff, students and parents (see Appendix 3 for a summary of the outcomes of these sessions) looking at areas such as wireless conectivity, IT support, staff training, Apple vs. Microsoft and how the MLE/VLE should operate.

The ICT User Group, which was chaired by the local authority ICT project manager along with representatives from the school and the governors, used this same structure with each stakeholder group – the teachers, the students, the local community and so on. This enabled me to bring together everyone's views under a series of common headings.

One response to the following question from a member of staff particularly stood out for me: If you had to state it, what would be your one dream for the use of ICT in aiding and developing learning?' The answer: 'We want to create a mobile theatre for learning.' I was really struck by the simplicity of the phrase and the depth of vision centred within it. It created a picture in my mind of how ICT would function in the school if we were successful. The word 'theatre' implied a place of curiosity and wonder. This was just what we were aiming for.

The primary learning point for approaching ICT in this way was that it translated the techno speak into a language we could all understand. From my own perspective, as a non-techie, it gave me the courage to challenge ICT experts on the basis of how far their proposed solution would support the vision of the school and how it would make a difference in the lives of young people. My strength was not in understanding blade servers or cabling, but in constantly bringing proposals back to the key question: how will it aid learning?

I am proud to say that I was clearly an irritant for some of the ICT professionals who had not been challenged in this way before. I found that many of the large ICT organisations that have been involved in providing technology to schools for a number of years seemed unable to articulate with any clarity how the technology they were promoting could actually enhance learning.

An enduring memory concerns one of the many 'competitive dialogue' sessions we attended as part of the tendering process for the contract. (For the uninitiated, a competitive dialogue is basically a series of conversations and presentations from each of the competing firms. It allows them all to have the same time allocation and a chance to listen to the school and come up with a solution.) Bear in mind that we had already issued them with our Learning Manifesto and a detailed ICT summary document in advance of the meeting, so were hopeful of a bespoke presentation that catered to the school's needs. How naive we were!

A presentation from one of the bidders started with a PowerPoint slide about 'blade servers' and went downhill from there! Children and learning were rarely mentioned. My complexion began to match the red suit I was wearing. I was fuming! How dare they waste our time and not listen to what we wanted or bother to engage in our vision.

As someone who finds it hard to hide my feelings, it soon became apparent that I was not at all happy. I sat through to the end of the presentation, upon which the speaker asked if there were any questions. 'Yes,' I replied through clenched teeth, 'where, if at all, do children and learning feature in your proposal?' After much coughing and shuffling, with anxious looks being exchanged between the presenter and their team leader, I received the response that they felt it would be necessary to have a 'below the table conversation' before we could have an 'above the table conversation' on this point.

Suffice to say, this firm was not above, below or anywhere near the table when it came to handing out the contract. The one that did, engaged fully in the journey we were on and wanted to provide the foundations for our castle in the air. That is not to say that it has been perfect, but compared to some horror stories I have heard about in Wave 1 of the BSF programme, we have done well. What's more, the closeness between our vision for ICT in the school and our Learning Manifesto meant that we always had something to refer back to when we felt the contractors had lost sight of it. Easy, really, when you think about it.

A final big tip for those of you for whom the build and ICT contracts are separate is to make sure they are congruent in terms of values and vision and, as near as possible, get the time scales of contractual work aligned. We had a three-month difference, with the ICT element trying to catch up throughout the project – a state of affairs which created some real headaches. This is where having a strong vision helped us to keep focused on where we were heading.

Once we felt that our survival needs had been met for the school's vision, we could move on to the next stage of development by tackling both the positive and negative aspects of tribalism in the workplace.

Checklist

■ **Do** ensure your school has a shared understanding of what learning is and how it should look. Use the stimulus for the project to broaden your establishment's thinking. Start from blue (or pink) skies and dream the undreamable. The further you push the boundaries at this stage the more chance you have of making a difference.

■ **Do** have a vision for learning that is driven by moral imperatives as opposed to the outside influences of government initiatives.

■ **Do** take the time to include all community stakeholders in the visioning process (and I don't mean just paying lip service). Plan real sessions that will capture the views of the community the school will serve. Choosing representatives from all interested parties and involving them in the visioning process will result in a robust vision that has support from most (it will never be all!) sectors of the school community. This will then become your backbone that will help you to drive your vision through.

■ **Do** ask questions like: What do I want the ICT to do? What experiences do I want students to have? What values do I hold dear, and how does this affect my practice? What should learning be like in an ideal world?

■ **Do** be creative and innovative, and keep going in the face of comments like, 'It can't be done', 'It's too expensive' or 'We just don't do it like that' (or anything to do with tables).

■ **Do** resist the lure of shiny toys or the latest gimmick and focus on what the technology can do for learners. Insist that ICT companies offer mechanisms to deliver *your* vision for learning in the bidding process. You will be bombarded by firms who will preach education but simply want to sell you the latest gadget or something they have stockpiled in bulk. You will be told what to have and what to do and what your vision should be. You will be amazed at the lack of educational understanding (or perhaps you won't!).

■ **Don't** copy what others have done. The same is true of the buildings and structures as well as technology. Adapt rather than adopt. Learn from the mistakes of others and find the best responses to your own context. Do not accept 'You can't ...' Anything *can* be done. The real issues are costs and consequences. These may not be as bad as you are at first told. Push the boundaries!

■ **Don't** let the nineteenth-century model of education restrict your imagination.

- **Don't** think of structures, think of activities.

- **Don't** ask yourself: What kind of ICT do I want? What sort of building do I want? What do others have? What do we do now?

- **Don't** accept off-the-shelf solutions if they are not right for your context.

Chapter 2

Science Isn't a Subject, It's a Philosophy

A bird doesn't sing because it has an answer, it sings because it has a song.

Maya Angelou

In Chapter 1 we acknowledged the importance of having a shared vision of what learning is and what it looks like. Common goals and values will drive your development forward and will be the accountability system to which your project must answer. Accepting all of that as a given, leaders also have to recognise that people may publicly sign up to a unified vision, while privately maintaining their old 'tribal' customs and rituals, which may or may not undermine the very goal to which you are striving.

There are many different tribes in a school: subject areas, faculties, leadership teams, senior leadership teams, pastoral staff, teaching assistants, administrative staff, science technicians, premises staff, catering staff, student support officers, the special educational needs team, cleaning staff, newly qualified teachers, community workers and governors. One school; so many tribes. All of these groups have their own rituals (cakes on a Friday, Christmas parties, moaning about the head) and their own identities (faculty logos, subject policies, office working practices). The positive side of such traditions is that it brings together – and bonds – a group with a shared view of the world. Their rituals and customs give them a collective identity, one that can be quite different from other groups in the school.

One of the negative sides of this tribalism is 'groupthink', where individuals imagine they are thinking for themselves but are simply going through an agreeable amalgam of thoughts that are coherent with what everyone else in the group is thinking. Such a homogenous reaction also extends, in times of significant change, to fear, so the tribe feed off each other's fears, concerns and imagined worse-case scenarios, triggering the 'fight, flight, freeze or flock' response at a deep neurological level.

One of the responses that you may find at your door as a particular tribe deals with their fears is that they will seek to undermine what you are trying to achieve. Ignore their undermining practices at your peril. Michael Fullan talks about the 'traitors' in our midst, while others call these people the 'well poisoners'. Tribalism is a reality, so don't try to fight it; but it does need to be dealt with in a positive way which will in turn strengthen the vision and determination of the school to carry on. In other words, embrace resistance as a way of generating new ideas. After all, if an institution does not have some resistance in its midst, it could be a sign of dangerous groupthink on a school-wide level – a sure fire sign of stagnation.

In his book *Leading in a Culture of Change*, Michael Fullan talks about the potential pitfalls of ignoring resistance:

> *Defining effective leadership as appreciating resistance is another one of those remarkable discoveries: dissent is seen as a potential source of new ideas and breakthroughs. The absence of conflict can be a sign of decay. Sometimes ... prolonged 'equilibrium is death' ... [so] allowing (even fostering) negative feedback is a step (not the only one) to needed improvement. (Fullan, 2001: 74)*

To encourage feedback, the head teacher set up a weekly drop-in session for staff, students, governors, parents and community leaders that continued for a number of weeks in the run-up to the design stage, so they felt they had some input into the design process. These were deliberately organised so different tribes came together in the same session, which although voluntary were well attended. In this way, several groups heard how each other saw the world and how their views related to learning. In particular, it was a chance to see how different groups' views of learning translated into the idea of our learning spaces.

I attended nearly all of the sessions and there were many light-bulb moments when individuals could see the possibilities of a new approach to a learning environment. I also witnessed many instances where people felt threatened and their survival behaviours began to surface in comments such as, 'So, where is my classroom?', 'Where is the staffroom?' or 'What about staff loos then?'

In learning to know other things, and other minds, we become more intimately acquainted with ourselves, and are to ourselves better worth knowing.

Philip Gilbert Hamilton

Also attending most of the sessions on the development of thinking during the tricky 'survival' moments was an educational consultant, Peter Scholey, with experience of Wave 1 of BSF. His input was vital in giving the senior leadership team (SLT) the confidence to carry on with their plans and with whom we could bounce ideas around. At the end of each session the group summarised the three key learning points that needed to be taken forward to the design process, thus giving the head and his team a clear steer as to what the staff felt was important when it came to learning.

An interesting outcome of these sessions was a rough design that showed how connected the various 'subject tribes' actually were and displayed the artificiality of what constitutes a subject in the first place. Who decided what Geography was? How did we end up with a subject called Psychology? As one of the teachers observed, 'Science isn't a subject, it's a philosophy'; in which case why do we need separate Biology, Chemistry and Physics subject leaders?

As you can imagine, questions like this were seen as a real threat by the teaching staff – they still are – and provoked instant tribal and survival behaviours. Our view, as an SLT, however, was that we had to keep pushing the boundaries of our collective thinking to see what could be possible. As Ian Gilbert observed in his article 'What If ...?' in 2004 (Appendix 6): 'What if more secondary teachers realised that, first and foremost, they were there to teach children not subjects?' As a result of such challenging thinking we did lose a few staff along the way, and that was fine. Some of those who were left were 'well poisoners' and would not have enjoyed the changed working experience in the new environment.

So, how else can a school bring people along on the vision that has been developed?

While the head teacher was directing consultation sessions with the entire school community on the new building, I was hatching a cunning plan on how to utilise the £2.1 million funding for ICT to support the human face of the whole change management process. By my logic, and from the messages we had received during the ICT consultation sessions, there was a need to address the whole range of survival-driven needs that the project would provoke as we addressed the changing twenty-first century environment; none more so than when it came to embracing new technologies. What was needed was a bespoke training programme for staff that would empower them to embrace the vision wholeheartedly – and take a few risks along the way.

What unfolded was a fascinating journey into the human psyche in which the school worked together with our ICT contractor, Mouchel, to develop a continuing professional development (CPD) plan that would involve one-to-one interviews with all staff (teaching and support), a person-alised teaching programme with learning outcomes and a ring-fenced budget from the £2.1 million that was three times the suggested amount of spending for CPD (I had been *advised* to spend just 5% of the overall budget on staff training, not the 15% I was intending to employ!).

Appendix 4 describes the CPD 'Learning Loops' developed by Independent Thinking associate Jim Smith, who was working closely with us on the project. It is a model through which new ideas are introduced, integrated quickly into classroom practice, reviewed and then improved. The impact has been powerful with staff. It was a key factor in enabling a smooth transition into the new building and it was a way for senior leaders to tap into each individual member of the school team and explore just how they saw learning.

Prior to the interviews, each member of staff had been asked to fill in an online questionnaire which asked them to reflect on their own skills. The survey included ques-tions relating to specific ICT expertise (how proficient staff members felt they were with software such as Excel, PowerPoint, etc.) along with pedagogic questions (how confident they were with aspects of teaching and learning such as group work, literacy and behaviour management).

It also asked staff to assess themselves on a sliding scale of feeling 'not very confident' in a particular area to 'very confident and could show others'.

I used the survey results during the one-to-one interviews, in which I would ask the same key questions:

To know where we are:

- If I were a fly on the wall what would I see in your classroom that made you proud?

- If you had the opportunity to lead on one aspect of learning in the school what would it be and why? How did you develop your skills in this area?

To know what is required:

- How do you think the expectations for learning in Nailsea School are changing?

- How can we take advantage of being in the new building to create effective learning opportunities? Have you any thoughts about how the new building might help you/us create effective learning opportunities for the students?

- How will this impact on you professionally? What changes might that fly on the wall see?

To have confidence in our competence, both now and in the future:

- How can the school best support your professional development?

This formed part of the process of staff coming to know themselves – their strengths, and limitations – and is a key element of the 'self' level of spiral dynamics (which is the theme for Chapter 3). Importantly, the survey not only asked *what* they wanted to learn but also asked them, in a way that modelled what we were expecting of them as teachers, *how* they wanted to learn so we could do our best to accommodate their personal learning preferences.

By going through this process and identifying how they as learners liked to learn, we put together like-minded groups centred around specific themes of development as well as certain learning styles. It also allowed the SLT to challenge misconceptions about the vision of the school in a personal and non-threatening way as well as enabling staff to express concerns – or positive comments – about the process to senior leaders. We gave each and every member of staff individual time, which was a significant investment in the staffing body and in their personal development.

What is more, we are still reaping the benefits of this work. We front-loaded the funding to the first two years of the BSF programme, so a personalised staff learning programme continues in the school today.

The ultimate measure of a man is not where he stands in moments of comfort, but where he stands at times of challenge and controversy.

Martin Luther King, Jr

A very good example of a tribe feeling threatened and not working well together occurred with the SLT about a year into the build programme. Due to the pressures of relentless meetings, tight deadlines and continual problem solving, the team had become fractured. It was split in half between the three members actively involved in the build programme and those who weren't.

The three staff involved in the build – myself, the other deputy and the head teacher – had our own special BSF vocabulary made up of acronyms such as competitive dialogue (CD), outline business case (OBC), Partnership for Schools (PfS), pre-qualifying questionnaire (PQQ), and so on. These meant very little to the other members of the team and as a result they felt threatened by their non-involvement on a day-to-day basis. Unfortunately, at the time, we felt powerless to do anything about it. We were hurtling along at a breakneck pace with not only the project to handle but, in my case, a teaching load and the other parts of my 'day job' such as timetabling, staffing, curriculum design and so on. It was the same for the head and the other deputy. Our workloads had not been adequately adjusted to allow for full commitment to the project. This meant, before long, we inevitably reached a point where, if we did not do something, the team would fracture irrevocably and the health of individuals would suffer.

So, we called in Roy Leighton from Independent Thinking to take us away for the day and try to bring us back together again. It was also at this point that he introduced us to spiral dynamics as a model to structure change. Although being taken through each stage of the 'spiral of human evolution' (see page 6) sounds disconcerting it meant that we could, as a team, begin to understand where we were individually and how we complemented each other. If all of us were operating at 'survival' level – the first stage of evolution – then our design for the new school would have been very functional and chiefly concentrated on what was needed for a school to operate (i.e. toilets, canteen, classrooms, places to work and play). Our aim, though, was to achieve a school design borne out of a higher level of human evolution.

We finished our away-day with a circle time session, where each member of the senior team took it in turns to state what they valued about each colleague. The effect was incredibly affirming at a time when we really needed support from each other. We all felt valued and ready to take on the next stage of the process. We could put problems within the team to one side, as there was less to worry about, and focus on the job in hand.

Roy followed this up with one-to-one sessions with each member of the SLT. This time the focus was on three important questions linked to three key human intelligence strengths – IQ (academic intelligence), EQ (emotional intelligence) and PQ (practical intelligence):

- ■ IQ: What ideas and new thinking have you and your team exposed yourself to that will assist in the development of effective teaching and learning at Nailsea?

- EQ: What have you done to engage, listen or challenge others and what has been the response?

- PQ: What actions have you and your team made to
  create systems, programmes or processes to build on
  teaching and learning at Nailsea?

What all this work added up to was a sense that we had
invested in the school's leadership in a powerful and practical way, and this had the dramatic effect of sharpening
our minds to better focus on the task in hand.

I recommend that any senior team engaged in such a
project should plan to go through a similar process as
soon as you get notification. I am not saying that we all
came away as experts in spiral dynamics; we did not and
that was not the aim. We did however come away with
a deeper knowledge of ourselves and how we interconnected as a team.

Checklist

- **Do** make sure you are aware of how you view the
  world.

- **Do** ensure you have evaluated the stage of evolution
  of the institution you lead (e.g. Are you all stuck in
  survival mode or still fighting each other as tribes?).

- **Do** be aware of the competencies, skills and deficien-
  cies of the SLT.

■ **Do** make sure you share what you value about each other and acknowledge what each of you brings to the team.

■ **Do** make sure you have a shared understanding of where your starting point for change is.

■ **Do** ensure you have the resources to hand now, at this moment, to address the change management needs facing the project by analysing what is needed and, if necessary, asking for help from outside the institution.

■ **Do** make time to look after yourself and the SLT – adjust responsibilities and build capacity to absorb the extra workload. Assign mentors to those staff who are most heavily involved in the design process and have away-days to reconnect with each other and the purposes of the project.

■ **Do** remember that the biggest fear factor for many of your staff will be the new ICT challenges. The ICT component is the most difficult element to get right in ensuring that it is effectively integrated into both administrative and teaching and learning practices. Have a clear concept of how you will use it to improve the learning experience. This may be more than simply the use of ICT in teaching. You can change working practices by introducing technological solutions to registration, planning and communications. Use the ICT training budget to train for change in teaching and learning pedagogy. Ask staff how they would like to learn and then give them training in that way.

- **Do** get key messages out to staff and students on a regular basis to involve them in the process. Communication lines need to be crystal clear.

- **Do** organise regular drop-in meetings; 'meet the head' sessions and stakeholder community events mean that there will a shared sense of ownership. It is very easy, however, to get so involved in the meeting cycle that SLT presence around school is compromised, leaving the staff feeling neglected. If the senior team looks after each other, there should be plenty of presence and energy to go round.

- **Do** remember that change entails anxiety, fear, anger and irrationality on behalf of staff, students, parents and governors.

- **Do** listen, talk to and reassure your staff.

- **Don't** let the pressures of a build project overwhelm you or assume that the leadership team structure can stay the same. Running a school and building a school are two very different tasks.

- **Don't** assume that what they say they are worried about is what they are really afraid of. One of the biggest fears will be about changes to working practices. This will be expressed as concerns about other issues (e.g. toilets, workload, where their room will be in the new building).

■ **Don't** be afraid to confront those who do not want to go on the journey with you. The organisation cannot run effectively when the traitors and well poisoners are allowed to go unchecked. Embrace their resistance – remember that 'equilibrium is death' – and use it as a chance to stimulate debate.

■ **Don't** keep developments to yourself in a well-meant but misguided attempt to protect staff and students from good or bad moments.

Chapter 3
Forming Relationships and Engendering Commitment

Knowing yourself is the beginning of all wisdom.

Aristotle

It should be becoming apparent by now that to end up with an educational project of which you are proud requires brave leadership. For leaders to feel brave, they need to have very firm foundations of belief to stand on – values founded upon their particular combination of principles and vision; not to mention great emotional intelligence and a healthy dose of wisdom. Another requirement for brave leadership is the knowledge of how your role fits into the grand(er) scheme of things – and then ensuring you have the freedom to go forth and show the way like a true leader.

Too often in school organisations, brave leadership is seen as a charismatic head teacher who takes ownership of all decisions and has to be referred to on everything, thereby leaving their senior leaders redundant from a leadership point of view, in effect reducing them to operational managers. As a result, their confidence is often eroded and their potential to expand their skills is cut off.

At the other end of the scale, you have head teachers who delegate many of the tasks to their senior leaders, have little to do with the direction of their work and then claim that, by giving the individual an opportunity to lead, they have shown pure genius. It is a bit like a parent throwing their child into the deep end of a pool and expecting them to swim without any direction. If the child learns to swim out of necessity and survives, then the parent is to be praised; if the child simply sinks, then the child was at fault for not being clever enough. To make matters worse, this type of head teacher also tends to meddle with the finished product, something which is infuriating for the person who had been simply left to get on with it in the first place.

Much has been written over the years about educational leadership, but leadership guru Michael Fullan succinctly summarises much of this research into five main components illustrated in the Framework for Leadership.

What I like about this diagram is the acknowledgement of the power of relationships, which are particularly important in a changing culture. This is an area that can sometimes get forgotten or left until last after the establishment of systems and processes. From my perspective, getting to know the people who work in your institution is the starting point for exploring the necessary leadership required to take it to the next level of its evolution.

Framework for Leadership

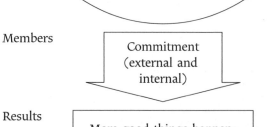

Leaders

Enthusiasm

Moral purpose

Understanding change

Coherence making

Relationship building

Knowledge creation and sharing

Energy

Hope

Members

Commitment (external and internal)

Results

More good things happen; fewer bad things happen

Source: Fullan, 2001: 4.

Effective leaders are highly skilled at building relationships with a diverse range of people and groups. In his book *Leading in a Culture of Change*, Michael Fullan says: 'They continually encourage purposeful interaction and problem solving, and are suspicious of easy consensus' (Fullan, 2001: 5). His work has made me focus on the importance of human relationships and the value of listening to people's stories. In doing so, people feel better understood and more involved.

That said, when leading a whole school rebuild it is clear that many styles of leadership will be needed at different times. For example, in times of crisis an autocratic, coercive style will be called for and at other times a more democratic approach will be required. The skill of the effective leader is in knowing which technique to employ at the right time.

Whichever type of leadership there is currently at the top of your school – and if you are a head teacher reading this then you need to reflect on the kind of leader you are – it is vital that under the relentless pressure of a school build programme all the key staff involved feel safe and secure in their role, and have accountability structures to which they can refer. This frees things up so there is more opportunity for the necessary bravery, courage and risk to take place.

Forgive me if this sounds obvious, but it is surprising how often this is not considered. When you are constructing a role for a member of the SLT, it is important they feel they have ownership of a project and something concrete to lead upon. This is not to say that they work in isolation, but that they have clear lines of responsibility and an awareness of how their role overlaps with the other members of the team.

For example, when it comes to teaching and learning there should be one unambiguous lead. Obviously, other members of the team with responsibility for areas such as Assessment for Learning, Gifted and Talented and National Challenge, will feed into this, but it is up to the head teacher to construct boundaries around and within which the SLT can meet to discuss all the relevant issues with honesty and clarity.

Another factor that leads to brave leadership is the head teacher making explicit their expectations of the team. This is about boundaries again. When an individual is aware of what is expected of them within certain time-scales *and* has defined areas of leadership, then you have a winning combination.

I recommend that each role within the senior leadership structure has a set of key performance indicators (KPIs). For example, a deputy head in charge of standards could have a KPI of achieving a 5% increase in attainment in 5A*–C by the end of a particular academic year, or an assistant head in charge of student support and guidance could have a KPI of raising attendance figures from 92% to 94% within a specified timeframe.

All of the KPIs should be interconnected and stem from the school improvement plan. However, by making expect-ations explicit to the SLT they know where they are heading and, more importantly, can be given the freedom to achieve the indicators in their own way. Bravery is being sanctioned and is therefore much more likely to occur.

The head teacher's role should be that of the tiller on the helm as well as the lookout onboard the ship. They should encourage, ask questions and do all they can to ensure that team members are feeling safe. This should start with assessing practical needs such as: Do you need an office? Is your teaching load right? Is the meeting structure working? Do we need fewer meetings – or even more? The emotional needs of different individuals vary widely so questions the head should ask might include: What takes you out of your 'comfort zone'? How do you feel when you are challenged but not overstretched? Where you are on this diagram (see below)? (If it is in the 'panic zone', then nothing innovative will take place, or if it does, it will be at the expense of someone's health.)

Comfort, Stretch and Panic Zones

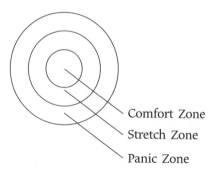

Comfort Zone
Stretch Zone
Panic Zone

Andrew Curran, a practising paediatric neurologist, in his book *The Little Book of Big Stuff About the Brain*, talks about the neurochemical dopamine as being crucial to the stimulation of learning. However, if we experience too much of this chemical the potential for learning shuts down and the brain goes into the 'fight, flight, freeze or flock' mode. One of the situations that can bring on this flood of dopamine is stress, and being placed well out of your comfort zone and into the panic zone is enough to do exactly that. As the good doctor says:

Stress is very good at releasing dopamine. There are however a number of problems to releasing dopamine in this way. Firstly: the dopamine released by stress is inclined to arrive in a great flood that bathes huge numbers of nerve cells rather than in the very specific point-to-point way that is ideal for specific template learning. Chronic stress over weeks and months can also theoretically lead to the loss of the ability to release dopamine appropriately. This failure of dopamine release may be the neurochemical burnout that is one possible explanation for conditions such as depression, chronic fatigue syndrome, and a variety of other psycho-emotional conditions. (Curran, 2008: 74)

Individuals who are placed in an area of stretch without appropriate support mechanisms in place will quickly enter the panic zone. They may become unable to function, make decisions rationally or manage their workload. In short they could be headed for a breakdown. Make sure that you give this individual time to express what is making them anxious; but also accept that you may not be the person they can speak to about this, because you are their boss, so perhaps you need to find them a mentor.

A mentor fulfils a different function to a line manger in that they do not pass judgement on an individual. Instead, they might offer coaching to extend their colleague's thinking, suggest advice from a position of knowledge and experience or simply just listen to their concerns as a sympathetic ear. Mentoring gives people space to discuss ideas as well as voice their fears. The impact of such a relationship on leaders in highly stressful projects is to maintain and build their confidence, and to ensure they get as much out of the working environment as they can.

It is no great surprise that many head teachers, business managers and other school leaders get signed off with stress; long-term sickness attributed to stress-related disorders is on the increase in the educational world. In 2005, the National Association of Headteachers surveyed 1,800 schools and found that more than a third of absence among head teachers was due to work-related stress. This was a 26% increase on the previous year (BBC News, 18 November 2005).

In 2007, the then National College for School Leadership (NCSL) conducted a research project entitled *A Life in the Day of a Headteacher: A Study of Practice and Well-Being*. In it, researchers looked into the factors that led to many head teachers suffering from stress-related disorders. They concluded:

Conducting this study has reinforced the urgent need for further empirical research into the ways in which contemporary headteachers carry out their role. This would allow thorough exploration and understanding of the specific and complex relationships between well-being, stress, job satisfaction and work–life balance. (Bristow, Ireson and Coleman, 2007: 11)

How then do we avert the tide of stress while at the same time asking more of our school leaders who may not necessarily have the skills or competencies to guide large build programmes?

Andrew Curran has a solution. After twenty years studying the major works on psycho-emotional care, which adds up to millions of dollars of research, he has come up with a very simple message:

UNDERSTAND the human in front of you. Then you will improve their SELF-ESTEEM. If you do this you will improve their SELF-CONFIDENCE. And if you do that, they will feel emotionally ENGAGED with what you are doing. (And remember, perhaps most importantly, that the human 'in front of you' is also yourself. Do you understand yourself? Are you good for your self-esteem? Do you improve your self-confidence? Are you emotionally engaged with yourself?) (Curran, 2008: 81)

Intellectual needs can be catered for by providing accessible expertise to SLT members. In my own case, I was lucky enough to be guided by an ICT consultant, Les Wharram, who translated the technospeak for me, as well as an ex-head teacher, Paul Kent, who was inspirational as a mentor in all things relating to leadership. He kept me focused on the myriad duties I had to discharge and enabled me to keep a perspective and prioritise.

Other ways to cater for intellectual needs include training days, visits to other schools, meeting an opposite number from another project or even having an e-mail relationship with a leading educational thinker to keep your moral purpose uppermost in all things. I was fortunate enough to have been introduced to the network of associates from Independent Thinking, so throughout the duration of the project I had access to educational speakers and thinkers, motivational gurus and practising teachers who had a vision of what learning could look like. More importantly, we all spoke the same language: the language of hope.

A leader is a dealer in hope.

Napoleon

To be given the opportunity to be part of a project that could potentially give hope to many thousands of children now and in the future is an awe-inspiring responsibility. By investing in the emotional, intellectual and practical needs of the leaders who have this responsibility bestowed upon them, the country will be left with a legacy of remarkable architecture that really does make a difference when it comes to young people's learning.

Checklist

- **Do** expect to be out of your comfort zone.

- **Do** get used to the feeling of being 'comfortable with feeling uncomfortable'.

- **Do** make sure that diagrams exist to show how the roles of the SLT overlap – this will keep people focused on their responsibilities and know who to liaise with.

- **Do** ensure that if, as a head teacher, you come to the realisation that you are not the person to be mentoring individuals in your team, you are big enough to accept it and provide someone else who can. A mentoring relationship is very different to a line management one.

- **Do** insist that the local authority/Department for Education provide funding for mentors as part of the capital rebuild programme.

- **Do** make sure that if, as a school leader, you have promised to do something, you do it! Trust is everything in this process. If it goes, it is very hard to get it back again.

- **Do** make sure that capacity is built in for local authority leaders. This is not just about the school; after all, the local authority is very often the client (i.e. they are the ones with the money).

- **Do** keep the thinking joined up. It is easy to separate the ICT from the building and the educational vision.

Different subcontractors talk different languages and have different approaches. Your role is to make sure that everyone is talking your educational vision/language.

■ **Do** remember that, when it feels like there is no light at the end of the tunnel, when staff and governors are getting cold feet and when people start to question the direction of travel, this is when brave leadership is needed. Return to the original vision, test decisions against that vision and, if they stand up, carry on with courage.

■ **Do** bear in mind that the most dangerous questions are the ones you didn't ask. At the start of the project get used to demanding explanations and details of the consequences of decisions that are being made. Remind the ICT and architecture experts that you may not know what they assume everyone knows – but they don't know how to run a successful school with 1,500 teenagers in it.

■ **Don't** feel like you have to know all the answers, and don't assume that everyone knows what they are doing!

Chapter 4

Conventional Toilets, Standard Classrooms

Knowledge of what is does not open the door to what should be.

Albert Einstein

From the moment Nailsea School received notification that the local authority was going to allocate the money for rebuilding a school to us, the BSF machine sprang into action. There were many planning schedules that were put together and used to guide us through the stages of design. The project for the build was steered by an outstanding project manager (Paul Gibbs), working on behalf of the council, who was very definitely a key factor in the success of the building. He was the very human face of project management yet ruthless in keeping the project on time.

What unfolded next was a relentless programme of planning meetings and scheduling. During the tender stages, when each architectural firm was bidding for the contract, the SLT were treated to visits to other schools to get a feel of what the company could offer. For example, the firm that was ultimately successful took us to Leeds to look at a school that had been rebuilt under the BSF scheme. Looking back at my notes nearly two and a half years later, I have written: 'I like the curves', 'outside stairwell – don't like it', 'conventional toilets, standard classrooms'. I was clearly looking for something different, and I wasn't seeing it. The vision we were working to was asking us to push the boundaries of how things could be different, to develop something that was a shift towards the incredible – a building that would change people's lives.

We did not take away many examples of real difference, but we did take with us plenty of ideas in terms of cladding materials and the use of colour. In fact, colour was one of our biggest learning points because of its enormous ability to affect people's moods. One school in Leeds had used an aubergine hue to paint part of their external elevations and the effect was dramatic. Firstly, it said that this was not a typical school, and secondly it had the air of a hotel or exhibition centre, which had the effect of making you feel differently about the building before you even walked in.

Once our architect had been selected, we embarked on the planning meetings and then began the real discussions about the design of a learning school. The architects, Aedas, were selected after a series of user groups had scored their suitability against a set of criteria. They covered areas such as deliverability and suitability for purpose as well as adherence to the vision. Members of the user groups included the SLT and local authority personnel as well as students, who had a say through the school presidents.

The meetings were attended by all the relevant representatives required on a build project – engineers, architects, builders, project managers, local authority officers, ICT specialists as well as the school staff. The meetings were often long – eight hours was not unusual – and were not always chaired as well as they could have been. This meant a lot of time was spent going round in circles.

I was not only attending the building meetings but the separate ICT planning meetings as well. This is not recommended as it meant that I was soon exhausted and not functioning at my best. Make a note of the following point and stick it up in your conference room: endless meetings do not encourage creativity! It was a punishing workload that led to my classes being neglected as well as my day job duties as curriculum deputy being squeezed in around the build project.

It was also a time of enormous pressure. At the same time as making sure we had the build and ICT programmes on track, the SLT were tasked with the usual responsibility of driving up standards. As part of my remit for teaching and learning, I focused on the process of learning (more on that in Chapter 5) as well as tracking the outcomes of students. I am not at all ashamed to admit that, at times, the pressure was almost too much for us. We did, however, learn a lot during that period.

In addition, the role of deputy head teacher in such circumstances meant that both myself and the other deputy were under great pressure from a variety of individuals who were questioning the way things were being led. Our job was to listen to their concerns and anxieties (and there were plenty of these), try to solve the ones we could, shelter the head teacher from the minor issues, but make sure that the key matters were brought to his attention. We tried to unify the school as much as we could.

We both kept a great deal to ourselves during the first two years of the programme, making a conscious decision not to share our worries with the rest of the senior team. In effect we were 'keeping secrets' from them, which led to the fragmentation of our working relationship (as described in Chapter 2). It also meant that we had to continually check our faith in the way things were being done. To say that this required enormous mental strength and perspective is an understatement. With tight deadlines and continual fire-fighting this was not always possible.

I will remember those two years as some of the most challenging and yet rewarding times of my professional career, not least of which was my working relationship with the other deputy, Steve Richards. We were the yin and yang of deputy headship! At times, we supported each other without having to utter a word: a knowing look or kind smile was all that was needed when things were getting tricky. He was fantastic at detail and logical thinking; I was the creative and emotionally intelligent one. A match made in heaven!

Planning for the new school continued unabated, but preparation for packing up the old school and the process of actually moving into the new building was vitally important too. This factor was particularly powerful and the head teacher was insistent that we had an opportunity to 'say goodbye' to the old school. Some staff had spent up to thirty years of their working life in the old buildings, as crumbling and decrepit as they were (the buildings, not the staff!). It was important for all of us to say farewell to the old walls which had housed thousands of students for half a century.

At the end of term, after the farewell speeches to staff, the head teacher played a montage of images from the old school and asked for a minute's silence. It was a very intense moment to be seated in the school hall knowing that this would be the last time a group of staff or members of the community would ever do so. It was a great way to end the term, and provided an air of expectancy for the start of the academic year in the new school in September.

We were given five additional closure days for the project and we took three in July, prior to the holidays, and two in September, added on to the standard INSET days. We had planned for a staggered entry of students in the first week of term and the head designed a 'treasure hunt' for staff to complete on their first day in to get them acquainted with the new campus. Not all staff took part (horse to water and so on), but those that did enjoyed it.

Then the students came in two years at a time. In this way, we engineered a smooth entry into the new school for staff and, importantly, gave them time to unpack. It was still messy and not all boxes were unpacked immediately, but it was a relatively painless move to the new building.

The ICT side of things, however, was another matter. The contract had been three months behind the build throughout, and although by the time we moved in it had caught up and was only six weeks in arrears, it still meant that on day one we did not have working computers or telephones. To make matters worse, on the second day after opening we had a break-in during which thirty tablet PCs were stolen – vital equipment destined for staff.

The whole of that first September was a blur to me. I battled hard to get systems up and running and we did finally get all the PCs, Macs and printers working. We even had some of the more 'exotic' technology working well, such as electronic swipe key cards; although exactly one month and one day after the move they suddenly stopped working and staff could not log into their work bases to get their teaching materials. It turned out the swipe card firm had set all cards to expire after one month. Needless to say we had strong words with that particular contractor. What did we learn from that 'hilarious' incident? No matter how well you plan, the unexpected will occur and you will simply have to deal with it.

As far as planning for the outcomes of the ICT strategy, I employed the Qualifications and Curriculum Authority

(QCA) documents that were intended to implement and review the curriculum of a school (see Appendix 5). This served to link the desired outcomes of the school with the new technology. Too often the ICT strategy is not sufficiently associated with desired learning outcomes and contractors get away with providing off-the-shelf solutions that are not always fit for purpose, let alone fit for the twenty-first century.

I believe that future bidders for multimillion pound contracts should be tasked with *contributing to raising achievement in schools*. It should be a KPI of the contract; and I don't just mean raw attainment scores. Their contribution should actually serve to promote aspects such as developing team work, creating independence in learning, giving individuals responsibility, enhancing global citizenship through web technologies, encouraging community involvement through connecting with hard to reach groups (e.g. travellers and other minority sectors) and other areas like business and community support groups, which we expect schools to deliver.

ICT has the potential to be a great leveller, but all too often we see a digital divide between the haves and have not's. If we put ICT in plain speech, explain how it can bring people together and then demand of everyone involved in the process that they all work to exploit technology's potential for *the benefit of the learners*, then we could tap into a global powerhouse, especially in terms of school improvement.

Checklist

- **Do** take ownership of agendas where possible.

- **Do** set time limits for meetings and chair proactively. Long meetings burn people out and do not lead to innovative thinking.

- **Do** choose who will attend the meetings amongst the SLT. It does not have to be all of the team all of the time. Spread the load amongst you.

- **Do** keep sacrosanct a 'sanity meeting' during the meeting cycle. This is a gathering of your core SLT people to make sure you all feel safe and secure and know where you are heading. Discuss the things that frustrate or please you in the process. Talk about who you think you can trust and how you feel about progress. This way you will feel connected and, even if you stray out of your stretch zone, you know that you can always call on your colleagues to help you get back on track again.

- **Do**, if you are the head teacher, give your team and yourself headspace. Divert funding to allow members of the team to 'act up' in your absence, thereby giving you time to work from home, attend meetings and generally get a perspective on a large programme. You could, of course, appoint a temporary assistant head teacher for the duration of the project to lighten the load on other team members.

- **Do** think about planning for support needed during the process; this could mean consultancy advice or extra administrative support.

- **Do** plan to 'say goodbye' to your old building.

- **Do** employ security staff during the first month of opening to ensure expensive ICT items are not stolen!

- **Do** double-check technological implications before moving in – and don't just assume that everything is alright. Maintain a sceptical eye.

- **Do** design desired learning outcomes for the ICT element of the project and link these with your school improvement plan. Then hold those responsible to it. Try to make it a KPI of the contract before you sign anything!

Chapter 5

I Think It Went OK but Not Really Good

Big Owl continued. 'Nothing,' he said, 'nothing is more dangerous than an oak when it is the only oak you have. If you try to solve the problem with the first right answer that comes your way, then there is no guarantee that you'll be solving it with the best right answer. You have to come up with as many right answers as you can and then – and this is the gilded rule of problem solving – evaluate second. You should fly narrow only once you have flown broad.

Ian Gilbert, Little Owl's Book of Thinking

If asked, most people could list at least one or two individuals who have made an impact on their professional lives. For me, Mick Waters is one of those people. I first heard him speak at a Leading Aspect conference in Manchester where our school was receiving an award in Active Citizenship. As I watched and listened to Mick speak, I noticed that he was presenting entirely without notes and, to my amazement, actually included young people in his talk where they spoke for themselves about their learning. He also referred to learning throughout his presentation; a refreshing departure from the constant focus on targets and processes from other people at the top of the heap.

When, in 2007, I heard that he had taken the job of Director of Curriculum at QCA I was delighted. It coincided, of course, with our school build programme, so it was a heady cocktail of dynamism and moral imperative that drove us to develop our new curriculum and approach to learning. Mick had given the curriculum back to the teachers, and there was real sense of freedom that we had not had before.

In Chapter 1 I described the school's Learning Manifesto and the way in which we had decided to construct our own language for learning after examining a whole range of teaching and learning approaches. It was a quote from Carl Rogers and Jerry Freiberg in *Freedom to Learn* that most struck a chord with me:

I believe that all teachers and educators prefer to facilitate experiential, meaningful, whole person type of learning rather than the nonsense syllable type. When we combine certain elements into one scheme – a prescribed curriculum, similar assignments for all students, lecturing as almost the only mode of instruction, standard tests that externally evaluate all students, instructor-chosen grades as the measure of learning – then we can almost guarantee that meaningful learning will be at an absolute minimum.

(Rogers and Freiburg, 1983: 37)

How, then, was I going to engage all of the staff in an exploration of what learning was? We had a golden opportunity to create a change in culture and ethos at Nailsea School, so how would we do it?

While all of the educational models I had examined had been proven to work, staff felt they wanted to utilise their own expertise and establish a model of learning that was not ready-made – rather like all the other aspects of the BSF journey up to this point.

As a deputy head in charge of curriculum and teaching and learning, I was encouraged by this. So, buoyed up by the Curriculum Review led by Mick Waters and the QCA, and with a mandate from the staff to explore thoroughly a new way of doing things, I strove forward into unchartered territory, feeling like a true pioneer. The Curriculum Tree (overleaf), which originated in QCA materials designed to help schools focus on the important ingredients for effective curriculum design, sums up my approach. Instead of just focusing on the knowledge required to pass exams, I also wanted to raise the importance of attitudes to learning as well as specific learning skills.

At the same time that developments were taking place at a national and school level, the local authority was adopting a county-wide model of teaching and learning called 'Critical Skills'. All primary schools in the Nailsea area had been trained in this pedagogical approach, so I invited the proponents of the strategy to our school to begin the process of exploration. The advisors we worked with, Tim and Andrea Sully, are two of the best authority

Nailsea School Learning Manifesto

How will you organise learning?

Use of
Technology

Themed
Curriculum

Reading

Mysteries

**Confident
Individuals**

**Successful
Learners**

**Responsible
Citizens**

**Learning
Activities**

Creative
Thinking

Enquiry

Social

Assessment
for Learning

(Skills)

Information
Processing

Problem
Solving

Communication

Reasoning

Motivated

Enterprising

(Habits)

Curious

Principled

Reflective

Resilient

advisors I have encountered. They combined a sound pedagogical and moral philosophy with integrity and authentic real-life practice in the classroom – and they get tangible results. To my great surprise and delight, the Critical Skills model spoke exactly the same language as I did. It emphasised equally the importance of skills, dispositions and knowledge in learning.

What I particularly liked about the Critical Skills Programme (CSP) was that it was not an off-the-shelf model of teaching practice. It was a philosophy of education with sound, practical strategies that could be adapted and moulded to a particular context. It provided a way of thinking that spanned the divide between pastoral and curricular areas of school life, while also offering a way to run meetings, involve people and improve communications within school. I blended our contextual work with this approach to arrive at a new curriculum design in Year 7 as well as introducing a strong focus on attitudes to learning. It was the philosopher's answer to the question about what is important in education.

CSP originated in the United States in 1981 as a partnership between education and business communities. It is based on four broad educational premises, which provide purpose in the classroom, engage young people in their learning, enable classes to run more smoothly, address curriculum targets and focus on quality work:

1. It is essential, for learning to take place, that a collaborative learning community is created in the classroom. The sense of community should lead to

teachers and students supporting one another in their search for solutions to problems.

2. By 'making learning real', students can engage with information on a need-to-know basis, apply it and make sense of the world around them.

3. Knowing what to aim for in terms of results of their work allows students to use all the required knowledge, skills and attitudes for a modern world. The challenges would be carefully designed by teachers to achieve this.

4. Problem solving through challenges can be used as the main teaching approach, with it being used in large groups or with individuals. Challenges give students a wider perspective on learning, and the chance to connect their learning together. It is learning with a clear purpose.

As a school we were delighted in the synergy between this model and our aims for our young people. What we also wanted to see, however, was proof of its impact in an educational setting.

We did not have to look very far. The Teaching Expertise website (www.teachingexpertise.com) quotes several cases where improvements have been made through adopting this pedagogic model. For example:

In 1992 the small, rural Gilboa-Conesville School in upstate New York was bottom out of the schools in its state district. Students were openly smoking pot in the school and vandalism was rife. The pass mark of senior students in English was

40%. In the summer of that year English teacher Peter Fox took Level 1 Critical Skills training. Within two years the students' average results had risen to 70% and by 1999 to 90%.

Schools in Jersey and England have reported similar improvements in student attainment levels and behaviour. In a Bristol action zone, annual discipline referrals fell from 231 to 26 in 12 months, while in Jersey, a study in 2004 by the late Professor Ted Wragg and his team from Exeter University on the impact of CSP on the island concluded that: 'The Critical Skills Programmeempowers teachers, enhances pupils' learning and is appropriate for its purpose of preparing children for adult life in the twenty-first century'.

Two further reports in 2005 reinforced this positive message. The first, also in Jersey, was by Serco Learning Consultancy and concluded that '[where] teachers were giving an emphasis to "Critical Skills" the accuracy of their assessments was high and pupils' standards were rising above the levels measured by tests in previous years'.

The second, by the University of the West of England, quoted an Ofsted inspection report which associated CSP with the development of 16 desirable qualities, including raising achievement; improving aspirations; sense of responsibility; development of problem-solving and ICT skills; sense of community and care; and greater parental involvement.

With hard evidence to back up the impact of the model, school and local authority representatives went on a 'learning raid' to Bradford Academy to see both the building and the Critical Skills model in action. On that trip it was decided that the authority and the school would work together in piloting the use of Critical Skills in Nailsea School.

We decided to train our Key Stage 3 Leaders of Learning across all faculties in the Critical Skills model. I also wanted to construct a 'transition curriculum' in Year 7 which would build on the experiences of our partner primary schools and provide a smooth entry into secondary school. The training began in September 2008 and we were lucky enough to have Pete Fox, one of the pioneers in the use of the pedagogy, to deliver our first session. Pete was an inspiration in that he spoke clearly and simply about the need to reduce the number of initiatives that bombard educational institutions, in particular the individual teacher in the classroom, thus freeing their capacity to take risks and experiment with teaching and learning. You could see the tension leave the faces of teachers as he spoke about the CSP model delivering on all the principal educational initiatives, including Assessment for Learning (AfL), Assessing Pupils' Progress (APP), Social and Emotional Aspects of Learning (SEAL) and Personal Learning and Thinking Skills (PLTS). Initiative overload was hopefully a thing of the past, and teachers could be confident they were covering the multiple demands of government programmes through one unified approach – at last!

To begin the creation of our new curriculum we selected subject areas within the Creative and Media Faculty (Art, Drama, Music and Media) and the People and Beliefs Faculty (History, Geography, RE and PSHCE). These were to be our trailblazing departments and I am indebted to the faculty leaders for being courageous and tenacious in the face of resistance from elements within their teams.

The first thing was to try to knock down the walls of subject boundaries. To do this we initially asked staff to tell us what they held most dear about their individual subjects. This was tribal behaviour at its most virulent. I had set aside three days in the summer term of 2009 to bring together the first two faculties and start doing exactly that. Naively, I had expected to spend the first day dismantling the subject boundaries and the next two days reassembling them around themes – but it takes a lot longer than a day to break down the dogma of the 1988 Education Act! We spent much more time on this than I had expected, but necessarily so. We had to make sure that most (not all) staff felt comfortable with moving forward. For the first day of our planning we asked Roy Leighton to lead the session, and his enthusiasm and integrity carried us along on a wave of possibility and opportunity.

To ensure that the teachers could see how CSP worked in primary schools, I organised trips to local schools and allowed our teachers to spend time with primary teachers in their classrooms to see it in action. It proved to be a very powerful experience for many of them.

The next aspect of curriculum creation was the design of a series of 'challenges' for students in order to develop the knowledge, skills and dispositions of learning that are a cornerstone of the school's Language for Learning as well as for the Critical Skills model.

The challenges we designed required pupils to:

- Read and debate the challenge description given to them

- Make explicit the measures of good quality work by which their product will be judged

- Think creatively

- Think critically by continually evaluating the value of each contribution against the quality criteria

- Make decisions on how to move forward

- Divide up the work across the roles within the team

- Establish a project timeline

- Work together or individually to complete the project

- Use resources in a creative way whilst researching their challenge topic

- Display their finished product in a variety of ways ranging from ICT to dramatic role plays

- Be prepared to take questions and have answers on their product from a variety of audiences – fellow students, premises staff, parents, community and business leaders

- Evaluate the success of their product against the measures identified at the beginning of the challenge

- Reflect on their own development by thinking about what they have learned, how they have improved their knowledge skills, and attitudes, and what the areas of further development are

What resulted from the collaboration of our two chosen faculties was a transition curriculum that made best use of the language of Critical Skills as well as the concept of challenges. We were ambitious and had Year 7 students working on a challenge within weeks of arriving in the new school, bringing together Music, Drama, Art, History and Geography around an excursion to Chepstow Castle. This school trip had been in existence for many years but this time, instead of just filling in a worksheet, students were putting on dramatic re-enactments, capturing images on digital cameras and exploring the tone of the visit by sketching pictures, as well as looking at historical facts. The results of the project were displayed in the new school atrium.

It had brought a tried and tested (and rather tired) trip alive and the student response was overwhelmingly positive. The CSP model encourages students to evaluate their learning in a constructive way, so instead of 'strengths and weaknesses' or 'positive or negatives', the model uses the phrases 'what went well' (WWW) and 'even better if' (EBI). In the spirit of Critical Skills, here are a few of the WWW's and EBI's from the students when evaluating this first challenge:

WWW

- 'Working as a team'
- 'We got to choose our groups'

- 'Going on a trip to see it in full life'

- 'I think mixing humanities and creative arts was a really good idea because you got the chance to look at medieval art, music and humanities. Also the medieval fair was a fun way of showing our work'

- 'Working with people from different primary schools'

- 'We all worked collaboratively together as a group and it was enjoyable doing the challenge in all different classes'

- 'Everyone helped and done their bit on the project and helped each other if they struggled'

EBI

- 'The challenge was a bit longer'

- 'Smaller groups'

- 'Teams were chosen for us'

- 'We had more planning time'

- 'There was more drama involved in the trip'

- 'We had a certain amount of time for each aspect of the project'

- 'I think it went OK but not really good. I think that only one person did it all but some of us helped a little bit'

- 'I would have preferred to have worked on my own and have more time'

Contradictory though some of these comments are (perhaps that just goes to reinforce the debate about offering a variety of learning experiences to accommodate children's different learning preferences), they were used to feed into the second challenge of the year, which was a decision-making task on the theme of Christmas. This too had a positive response from the students.

It is also worth noting that we gave each student their own Learning Journal. This was used to capture their thoughts and reflections as they worked though the challenges throughout the year and reinforced the reflective and metacognitive aspects of the process.

In terms of the structure of the curriculum time, I designed the shape of the curriculum around the CSP idea of 'Check in' (introduce), 'Check up' (how are we feeling at this point?) and 'Check out' (what have we learned? Let's celebrate success). Across a fortnightly timetable, I scheduled double lessons for the whole of Year 7 at the same time. I had a 'check in' on Monday, week 1, periods 1 and 2, a 'check up' on a Friday afternoon in week 1 and a 'check out' either side of lunch on the last day of week 2. In doing so, teachers had the freedom to come together in a range of new spaces in the school campus and students could become part of the 'learning loops' (see Appendix 4).

The design of the new school building meant we had a variety of learning areas including three lecture theatres of various sizes as well as break-out spaces and more traditional learning spaces. It was wonderful to watch the learning take place in the new building and to see the areas being utilised just as we had envisaged them three years previously. I found the first year on the new school campus an emotional one; we had worked so hard to get it right that to see it working was extremely gratifying.

At the heart of CSP is the concept of building a 'collaborative learning community'. To leave this as the sole responsibility of the curriculum would be to do only half the job. Since adopting the model, I have used the techniques to build community in the way we run meetings, in the way I have set up the tutor programme and the development of communities in our newly introduced vertical tutor groups.

So what is the key when it comes to creating a real learning community – one built on trust and collaboration? In his book *Leading the Learning School*, Colin Weatherley suggests that communication is essential to success:

Communication systems are the means by which an organisation's real values (as opposed to publicly professed ones!) are translated into practice. In effect, they represent the 'specific observable behaviours' which show an organisation's values in action. Therefore, in a learning school, communication systems have three functions:

■ **The instrumental function** – *that is, giving and receiving information as clearly and unambiguously as possible ...*

■ **The intrinsic function** – *that is, motivating people by demonstrating that they and their ideas are valued ...*

■ **The learning function** – *that is, enabling people to collaborate effectively in tackling problems and developing policies ...*

[In] a learning school teachers need to be 'continuing learners' themselves ... As with their pupils, therefore, teachers need to be able to develop their understandings through performance, *that is, by 'learning with and from each other' in collaborative staff and school development sessions.*

(Weatherley, 2000: 121; emphasis in original)

This way of thinking about communication sums up what I feel is necessary not only during a complex build programme, but also if a healthy, functioning school is the desired end result. The communication lines within Nailsea were not as good as they could have been at times, due to the pressure of the work; however, the senior leaders showed themselves to be 'continuing learners' at all times. The development of the curriculum and the embedding of key pedagogic skills are still ongoing, but as you will see in the Quality Mark report quoted in Chapter 6, the use of the build project to kick-start debate and experimentation in teaching and learning has been recognised as a good thing. It would also, I hope, make Einstein happy.

It is in fact nothing short of a miracle that the modern methods of instruction have not yet entirely strangled the holy curiosity of enquiry; for this delicate little plant, aside from stimulation, stands mainly in need in freedom; without this it goes to wrack and ruin without fail.

Albert Einstein

Checklist

■ **Do** remember that it is not the new building that will raise standards; it is the change in working practices. This can start at the beginning of the project, before any sod is cut. If you haven't made progress by the time you move into the building it may be too late.

■ **Do** your research – and remember to cater for the intellectual, practical and emotional needs of the staff who are involved in driving through the change.

■ **Do** take the opportunity, in the years prior to moving in, to redesign the curriculum to maximise the new resources you will have. Focus on the vision for learning that you have developed and use the process to bring all staff on board for the journey. Remember that not everyone will want to come with you. This is OK. Let them go with good grace and dignity.

■ **Do** provide planning time for staff who will need more than a day to break down the walls of the National Curriculum.

■ **Do** regularly review how things are going.

■ **Do** use your trailblazers to lead others into the unknown.

- **Do** show yourself to be a lead learner; by trying, failing and recovering you show great integrity.

- **Do** see it as a chance to bring a sharp focus to learning and standards, to grab the moral imperative and drive through positive changes.

- **Don't** see the project as additional and separate from the 'day job'.

Chapter 6

No, Really, Where Will I Do My Pineapples?

Now, I don't want you thinking that everything in the Nailsea School garden is rosy, because it isn't. We have made great strides in the use of different learning spaces and we have embarked on a journey of exploration into redesigning the curriculum. We have also worked hard on minimising 'initiative overload' by using one key driver for school improvement, namely Critical Skills. On top of that, our exam results have increased to the best ever in the school's fifty-year history.

But if you ask me, 'Have you succeeded in transforming learning across the school?', then the answer is no, not yet.

If you ask me, 'Have all of the community taken this on board?', I would have to answer unequivocally, no, not all of them.

The crucial point, however, is that we have *begun* the process of change. To put this into context, before we moved into the new school we had three major obstacles to overcome in our quest for transformation.

The first was that the moral imperative that is in every school – the desire to improve children's life chances and outcomes – was buried very deeply under the need to protect the status quo and not make life too hard for teachers. Staff had spent a long time in substandard buildings with poor ICT facilities and had limited risk taking and creativity in their practice. Over the years, this had led to traditional teaching techniques becoming the norm (chairs and tables in rows, teacher at the front, teacher talk, very little ICT used in learning, an emphasis on teaching not learning). There were a few valiant souls who tried hard to break out of this. I remember, for example, an excellent young science teacher creating a wonderful student 'particles' dance, which was filmed and used during a staff INSET. I also do not want to decry all the staff who came to my 'Danger and Excitement' group in which we shared a few mad ideas about teaching and learning. We also had a coaching scheme to link up members of staff to share ideas.

It wasn't that the school was not interested in or closed to new ideas, but the default position was one of traditional methods. Attempts to change these practices were sometimes met with the response: 'Why change things, we are doing OK, aren't we?'

By using the BSF process as an opportunity to go back to basics and examine the reasons why they entered the educational profession in the first case, we reignited some teachers' flames of passion, fed more fuel to lights that had burnt a little low and gave plenty of room for the fully stoked bonfires to rage. Inevitably, the effect of this revisitation to the moral purpose was short term, which is why it is so important for school leaders to return to the *why* question in education.

Secondly, alongside traditional, default methods (driven by survival imperatives), there was an obsession with subject content and subject protection (driven by tribal imperatives). This is understandable due to the original National Curriculum which was heavily prescribed and provided schemes of work that teachers were expected to deliver. Teaching staff had become reliant on guidance from above and, to a certain degree, had lost their questioning capacity and, along with it, their creativity. As a result, at the same time as feeling straight-jacketed by the curriculum, they derived a sense of safety from following the guidelines. Add to this the inspection regime and you have the ball and chain that most teachers would say stifles their creativity and freedom.

But this does not have to be the case. This was a huge obstacle to overcome, chiefly because these limitations are largely in people's minds and do not exist in reality. Examination syllabi and Ofsted frameworks are often viewed as a barrier to innovation, as well as a crutch to lean upon. This can result in the reduction of pedagogy to a tick-box exercise if not viewed in a different way. Syllabi give you *what* students should learn, not *how* they should learn.

Ofsted frameworks capture practice in schools and are looking for educational progress in young people. If a school is achieving great results in a way that is different to another successful school in the next town, then both schools will be viewed in a positive light. This is hard for some staff to take on board or even believe due to the importance placed on Ofsted judgements, and it is easier and safer to stick to what they are told to do. So how did we overcome it? The truth is, we didn't completely, but we moved some of the teachers' thinking along.

And don't assume that it will be necessarily the more experienced staff who feel this way.

I remember at one stage in our curriculum redesign we were looking at a particular point in the academic year and were discussing how we could construct a challenge to bring together the arts and humanities subjects. A young member of staff in their second or third year of teaching said suddenly: 'Hang on a minute! We can't do the challenge there, that's where I normally do pineapples as part of still life!' With panic rising in her voice she wailed, 'Where will I do my pineapples?' So we spent some time exploring what it was the students were hoping to learn from their study of pineapples, and whether we could do it in a different way. We got there in the end, but I don't think we ever truly convinced that particular member of staff.

By focusing on how young people learn, we began to shift the teachers' thinking, however, it is very hard to encourage people to 'unlearn' learnt behaviours.

The obsession with subject content, knowledge acquisition and passing tests has, of course, been encouraged by our examinations system. The introduction of BTECs and Diplomas has been a good move towards valuing equally skills and knowledge. BTECS are widespread in use in some parts of the country although the Diploma qualification is now under question. The publication of the Wolf Review has thrown greater debate on the appropriateness of vocational education and how much of an 'applied' diet of learning should be given to students who are post-14. Technical academies, along with the concept of studio schools, could replace the previous government's approach to a personalised curriculum from 14 to 19.

Schools must be careful not to replicate the divide between academic and vocational students, that existed in previous generations, with less value placed on the latter; we have come too far as a nation to allow such devaluing to take place. We need to make sure, however, that we address the requirement for a complex personalised curriculum that serves the needs of individuals as well as the economic needs of a nation; one which is based on equivalence and value.

To make myself clear on the matter of subject content and knowledge, I am all for knowledge; ignorance is a terrible thing. What I do not support is knowledge for knowledge's sake. It is, of course, important to know key facts; they are required in order to learn to read and write and understand processes. Knowledge is also important in cultural awareness and for understanding the world in which we live. There is no merit, however, in acquiring a large bank of facts and figures in your mind, and yet do nothing with them. It was the Buddha who said: 'To know and not to use is not yet to know.'

We have to move away from the false premise that it is *either* knowledge *or* skills that should prevail in educational practice. We need not throw any babies out with any bathwater if we take a good long look at what is working and what is not. Furthermore, I would argue that the binary distinction between knowledge and skills is erroneous; it is the triumvirate of *knowledge, skills* and *dispositions* that will lead to effective learning. All three have equal value.

The third obstacle Nailsea School met on its journey to transformation was that, due to a demographic dip, the school was experiencing a fall in rolls. This had a serious impact on us in terms of finance and, as a result, we went through a restructuring exercise to scale down the school. This, of course, meant that people were forced, once again, back into their tribal and survival states, defending their roles and their subject areas. This meant that all our hard work to break down subject barriers was now under threat. We counteracted this setback by continuing with our programme of school improvement, utilising the BSF ICT funding to provide a first-class CPD programme to train up staff as well as continually and consistently reinforcing why we were doing what we were doing.

As we come to the end of our first year in the building, is it still as wonderful? Have the traditional methods begun to change? This is what we are seeing now:

- Greater use of ICT in classes.

- Traditionally 'non-techie' staff using laptops to help students learn as well as using eBeam (a technology that captures surface writing and saves it directly to a computer – it can then be projected onto any flat surface, such as a wall or table).

- Different spaces being used to enhance learning and experimentation with the layout of tables and seating in classrooms.

- Learning being more visible to more people – at staff bases or student areas, such as break-out spaces or open-plan rooms.

- Students being given the freedom to use mobile technology in break-out areas and to work on things they have chosen to do.

- Vibrant, real-world learning utilising Critical Skills methodology.

- Strong community engagement.

- Cleaner toilets.

- Less graffiti.

- Stronger student engagement.

- Staff and students beginning to use our Language of Learning and Critical Skills vocabulary.

But, of course, we haven't cracked everything (yet). We still see:

- Tables in rows in a few learning spaces.

- The teacher at the front giving didactic instruction. (To be fair, there is a place for this, just as long as it is not for the whole lesson!)

- An emphasis (but less so) on content delivery.

- Some tribal behaviour in subject areas and an unwillingness to change routines (e.g. setting in English).

- Greater concern for the needs of teachers than for the needs of students in some areas (e.g. Why create a sink-group that no teacher would want to teach? Why does the reporting cycle fit the teachers and not students?).

- Children being put – and then left – outside classrooms while the teacher carries on with the lesson.

- Teachers who are risk averse.

It will take some time, but the pendulum has begun to swing in the right direction; an energy has been created as well as a sense of curiosity as to how far we can go and how we can change things for the future. With such an attitude growing amongst the staff we are starting to feel more positive about the question of sustainability. We also have to remind ourselves continually where we have come from and how far we have travelled. I chaired a recent meeting where all the faculties had agreed to come together to work on a themed curriculum for Year 7, which would include all subjects. A year ago, this would have been unthinkable.

And we still have targets that we have not yet begun to meet:

- A unified community where *all* staff see it as their responsibility to identify good behaviour and challenge poor behaviour.

- Subject areas not only working together on a theme but really collaborating in the learning process and going deep into the overlaps.

- A post-16 curriculum that can offer Level 2 courses – a real imperative for the next decade.

- Embedding the Critical Skills model so it is the norm to speak our Language of Learning.

- Rolling out the Year 7 curriculum into Year 8.

- Making all staff ICT literate and seeing greater use of mobile technologies, including hand-held devices (something that has proved effective in enhancing boys' literacy).

- Greater interactive use of eBeam technology (e.g. so students can make their tables interactive and let the technology capture the thinking process).

- Providing all staff with a tablet PC which connects easily to projectors around the school and enables them to showcase pupils' ICT work. This would also help to move the teacher away from the front of the class to the side, thus removing them from centre stage.

- Full integration of card technology. We wanted to achieve an integrated card system to allow parents to credit money to a student account to pay for trips, food, equipment and printing. We were 'over-promised' on this (grrr!), but we are slowly making progress.

Let me take you back to the priorities document against which we were going to measure our success, certainly in the ICT project (see Appendix 5). We set out three clear priorities for our students, with specific measurable targets. The 'design and implementation' and 'review' sections show what was implemented and assess how successful we have been.

In terms of examination success, we have done extremely well. The school has raised the expectations of students and staff, and now achievement is rising too. We secured a 10% increase in 5A*–C passes at GCSE in the summer before we moved into the new school, to 74%. Subsequently, we went on to achieve an even greater increase after the first year in the new school with an impressive 81% at 5A*–C, which was an increase of 7% on the previous year and the best set of results ever. Our A level results were also good with 29% at A*–A, 61% at A–B and 79% at A–C. Our target for 5A*–C at GCSE was 80% and for A level were A*–A at 25%, A–B at 50% and A–C at 75%. So we achieved beyond target in both sets of results.

As regards the targets for creating independent learners, this is harder to measure, although our academic success is an indicator of this. In addition, the number of students using ICT in an independent way around the school demonstrated a freedom and responsibility that we had set out to encourage in our young people.

With respect to behaviour and community-building, there was a marked improvement when we moved into the new school although, as with any institution, this must be maintained and sustained. We achieved recognition of our use of the concept of community in raising standards and developing a vision through a Leading Aspect award called 'Using the Community to Raise Standards and Build a New School'. This involved a visit by the lead verifier, Ian Gyllenspetz, and it was apparent pretty early on during the verification day that we were impressing our visitor. We could clearly demonstrate how we used not just the *physical* external community in our visioning process, but also the *concept* of community in the deployment of Critical Skills in our school organisation.

Another big success of the project to date has been the strengthening relationship between the local community and the school. It has been wonderful to watch Nailsea Musicals, a private theatre company, hiring our facilities for stage shows and the local sports clubs competing over who can hire our new fourth generation rubber crumb pitch (the only one in the world, I'm told). Primary schools also use our sports facilities and local businesses have staged a community showcase in our school buildings.

Similarly, Partnership for Schools visited in July 2010 and commented on the maturity of the atmosphere in the school. It did not feel as if it had been open for only one year, they observed, as the sense of community was strong and great community practices were embedded. During their visit, I was asked how important, on a scale of one to ten, a 'vision' was to the overall success of a project. Ten out of ten seemed an understatement!

The school also received external praise and recognition when the verifier for the Quality Mark in Basic Skills visited in December 2009, just four months after moving in. He was very impressed and in his report commented:

The school leadership has been innovative in ensuring that the school vision focuses on the quality of learning and that it is clearly visible in the actions of staff and students, the curriculum, teaching and the learning environment. This holistic approach is starting to bear fruit. By involving staff, governors and students in this process there is a greater sense of ownership of and commitment to this vision. The school improvement plan reflects this change with a major focus on improving learning. Monitoring and evaluating is rigorous, the governors playing their part as critical friend.

A significant part of this focus on learning has been to provide a stimulating environment that matches the vision. I deliberately left this until last as this wonderful new school building can tend to dominate your thoughts on your tour, and I did not want the hard work of the school to be lost in the admiration for the building. Make no mistake, it has made a significant difference but only because the leadership has ensured that learning led its development not vice versa. It provided a new starting point for learning for this community. The head's input at the design stage cannot be underestimated. The design aids student interaction, shows learning as something to be shared and nurtured and provides space and facilities that support the vision. The really good thing is that it will continue to grow and develop because the vision for learning will not let it stand still. It is there to be enjoyed and be proud of and everyone is! The basic skills are more than secure here.

After so much hard work and effort it was nice to be appreciated!

It really hit home what we had achieved when I attended a Rotary dinner hosted in the school building. A Rotarian was asking me about the design process and how we had achieved the finished product. I began to explain the visioning process and she stopped me and said: 'But that's just it. I can't get my head around how you came up with the idea for this in the first place! It is beyond my understanding.'

I have to say that before we started the process, it was beyond mine too.

Checklist

- **Do** establish the non-negotiables for your school. What is, or is not, acceptable in terms of behaviour, uniform, staff dress code, the way in which we speak to each other, respect for the environment?

- **Do** publish the non-negotiables in every classroom or learning space.

- **Do** return to the vision regularly as a staff body and school body. Are we living up to it? Review progress and use the findings to feed back into the learning about the building.

- **Do** make sure you have time to 'road test' the tablet PC or mobile technology for staff and students. We ran out of time and it meant that momentum was lost and part of our vision for hand-held technology was delayed.

- **Do** be clear about the software needed for staff on their laptop/tablet.

- **Do** make projector connections swift and easy.

- **Do** make good friends with either your local authority ICT project manager or ICT contractor. You will need to work closely together to get anywhere near a coherent solution.

- **Do** make sure that you capture staff responses to the new building at least six months after you have taken up occupancy. They may surprise you. One member of staff said they felt 'lonely' in the new building, and that while the high visibility that glass provides was good for learning, it meant no privacy for staff in their work bases.

- **Do** provide opportunities for staff to share their successes and failures in using new technologies. We held daily staff briefings in the first month of moving in to capture concerns as well as positive comments. The concerns were nearly always about ICT!

- **Do** ensure that, if there are delays in the implementation of ICT, there are clear lines of communication to staff to explain why.

- **Don't** take the pressure off the ICT companies once you are in. Be prepared to withhold payments if the solution is not performing up to standard.

Appendices

Appendix 1
A Beautiful School

Nailsea School's vision is to be an 'Inspirational Learning Hub for the Community' where children and young people benefit from:

- *Progressive* teaching exploiting the Technology and Media Arts specialism

- A *secure*, *supportive* and *stimulating* learning environment

- A *collaborative* learning community, inspiring individual success

- *Inclusiveness*, providing opportunity for all to succeed

- Traditional *values* which build maturity, responsibility and tolerance

The school will be organised around learning zones incorporating groups of subjects or faculties, which are subdivided for managerial purposes into KS3 and 14-19. Subject areas may change their allegiances in the future and are of relatively low profile to minimise the artificial boundaries between areas of knowledge/understanding and to emphasise the unity of learning. We do not expect the KS3/14-19 split in faculties to be represented in the built structures, but we will allow for fluidity in subject allegiances. Learning will be focused on transferable skills and the development of the student's capacity for learning.

The Information, Advice and Guidance (pastoral) structure will be developed around mixed-age learning groups of about twenty students and one tutor. They will meet informally for discussions and seminars, but registration will be done electronically through proximity readers on entry into zones/classrooms or the school. This will help to ensure security and enable differentiated access to various parts of the buildings. It will also enable student arrival at different times of the day to take account of age, learning needs, specialised curriculum provision and so on.

The learning environment will provide a variety of spaces to accommodate a range of learning activities/experiences with integrated ICT resources. Spaces will communicate with each other visually while providing acoustic separation (e.g. between circulation spaces, lecture theatres and enclosed learning spaces). Colours and imagery will be used to define areas and the learning that is associated with them. One guiding principle for learning spaces is that they should reflect the world of work (e.g. business/ICT areas should 'feel' like an office/business environment). Catering facilities should be as one would find in a commercial setting. Our Media and Technology focus will be reflected throughout the built structure as it is in the curriculum experience of the students. A 'media studio' for use by all areas of the school will provide a focal point for this provision.

Learning and student services will be accessed on a 'service' basis. Student services (careers advice, mentoring, learning support, counselling, finance, health, parent support advisors, etc.) will be available as required from a central area. Locality teams, Connexions and other external agencies will have office space in this area to facilitate joined up care for the students and their families. Learning resources, including 16+ learning resources, will also be accessible from a central area, which has a high profile within the school. This area will have a strong media and technological ethos.

Catering/refreshments will be available throughout the day from cafeteria-style outlets. Fresh water will be available in learning spaces. Toilet areas will be distributed around the buildings in small clusters of cubicles with communal hand washing facilities open to the circulation spaces to restrict enclosed spaces to a minimum. Internal and external spaces provide social spaces for play, conversation and relaxation.

All students will have their own locker (built into the circulation spaces) and all students will have their own mobile electronic device (similar to a PDA or ultra-mobile PC) which will enable connectivity to e-mail, intranet, internet, their own workspace and enable teachers/tutors to download work to them. It will be their notepad and diary/organiser enabling them to have a single location for their records of learning, worked examples, assessment projects and so on. If possible it could also provide students with the facilities currently offered by devices such as Qwizdom.

Learning zones will each have resource bases for teaching and non-teaching staff that will provide quality accommodation for multi-disciplinary groups of staff and promote networking and staff development. Staff will have their own lockers in these bases for personal effects. Each resource area will have a mixture of social space, desktop area and computer workstations to enable a variety of activities to take place, which staff share depending on the activity they are undertaking. There is no central 'staffroom' in the building, with all staff accommodated in the learning zone bases. Passive supervision will be enabled by visual continuity with the spaces around them and clear lines of sight. Administration and senior staff offices will provide similar supervisory and role-modelling functions.

Staff training will be facilitated through the design of learning spaces. The high visibility of learning within the spaces will allow non-intrusive observation of lessons. At least one learning space in each learning zone will have audio-visual (CCTV?) facilities that allow lessons to be recorded from several camera angles and for this to be screened in a viewing room. In this way staff will be able to observe their own lessons, assess their development needs, teaching/learning strategies for groups and so on.

Community use of the campus will be for childcare, all age learning, social, leisure and recreation. Access to the sporting and leisure facilities will be mainly twilight and weekends and will include all-weather pitch facilities and running track, sports hall and grass pitches (on Golden Valley site?) and changing rooms. Lecture theatres will enable cinema and theatrical productions as well as community group meetings. Other use of the facilities will include conference facilities, after-school clubs (e.g. Orca Kids Club), adult learning, family care (e.g. counselling) and an internet cafe.

During the day adults from outside the school will access certain areas (e.g. conference centre) and community resources (locality teams, Connexions, etc.) as well as the Weston College Vocational Skills Centre. Students from other schools will use the Weston College Vocational Skills Centre and regional training centre.

Throughout the school the ethos of a vibrant learning community will be a visible reality. Learning and learners will be celebrated through the displays and the architecture.

Reproduced with the kind permission of
David New and Peter Scholey

Appendix 2
A Day in the Life of a Year 8 Student (2010)

8:00   After dumping my stuff in my locker and changing into my 'inside shoes', I go straight to breakfast, registering electronically on arrival in my learning village. While sipping hot chocolate I text my tutor to let him know I have an issue to discuss. He will give me an appointment for later on that day. Sometimes I respond to a text message from him. My tutor is a teaching assistant, but my best friend has a tutor who is a teacher. Even the head teacher is a tutor to one of my mates. Using my mobile I check my e-mails and download some homework to my teachers.

8:30   Having finished breakfast, and met up with my friends, I make my way to my first learning experience of the day. Today it is Maths/Science so I walk across to that zone. This learning area allows me to work collaboratively, in or outside the space, sitting comfortably in a group to discuss and plan how we are going to tackle a particular topic. Sometimes a group of teachers introduce the subject area to the whole group in the lecture theatre. Then we choose how to achieve the specified learning objectives, what technology we will need to use and whether to work independently or with others. For this topic I am working independently. I discussed this with my learning mentor for this area, and she agreed that I had valid reasons. We talked about the learning resources I would need and what evidence I would need to give to show I had achieved my learning objectives. We will also work together to assess whether I have achieved my objectives at the end of the topic. If I get stuck I can always ask her for help, but as I am very good at Maths/Science I often get to coach some of the others in the group.

10:30   I meet up with my tutor and a couple of my 'learning family group' for coffee. My tutor checks that I am happy with the way things are going and I talk to him about the issue that I have. Looking out onto the quad I see another couple of my learning family who are having a drink, while others are using the wireless network to e-mail their friends. Usually I play football on the communal pitch, but today I needed to meet up with my tutor. When it is raining I try to get into the internet cafe, but it is often crowded when it is wet. Some of the students are only just arriving at school as they are on the 'Day B' schedule, which starts and finishes later. I learn best in the mornings, but my older sister is not a 'morning person' so she comes in later. Not only does this help her learn

better, but also, Mum says, it saves a lot of argu-
ments in the mornings!

10:50 Now I am going to the enrichment part of my day.
I have chosen to do Creative Arts this term but
some of my friends have chosen Extra Maths, and
some are doing the 'healthy living' focus so they
are doing 'Food' and 'PE'. I did that last term and
it was very good.

12:50 'Day A' lunchtime is an opportunity for socialis-
ing and spending time in one of the canteens
around the place. I meet up with some of my mates
and we are all looking forward to the evening lecture. Our 'Thematic Learning Co-ordinator' is
bringing in Professor Kevin Kelvin as a keynote
speaker for our project on robotics. We are all very
excited about this and have a couple of hours off
this afternoon to allow time to chill at home so we
are alert for the lecture.

17:30 The robotics lecture is great. About 120 of us
packed into a lecture theatre to listen to Prof.
Kelvin. He is fantastic, and really inspiring. I
must make an appointment with the careers person from Connexions to find out how I can get a
job in robotics.

19:00 My Mum said I can spend an hour in the media
suite before going home, to work on our website
with my mates. Because I have done three extra
hours in school this week – with the lectures and
everything – I can go to school later tomorrow.

20:30 I only have one piece of homework to get done tonight. I download the work from the school's website by logging on to the lesson it was set in: twenty questions on how to make a play more dramatic. This one is easy, and by tomorrow the computer will have marked my work and told me what I need to focus on to improve. The wireless network means that my sister and I can both use the internet at the same time.

Reproduced with the kind permission of
Trudy Jones and David New

Appendix 3

Summary of Building Schools for the Future ICT Consultation Sessions

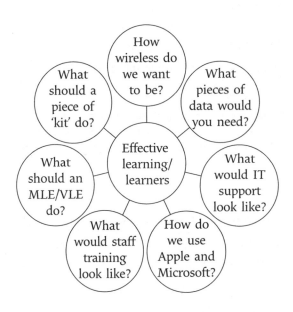

What should a piece of 'kit' do?

- Ability to communicate in many ways: Bluetooth, e-mail, internet.

- Speedy swipe or wave registration with credit to buy food or maths equipment, so no one goes hungry at lunchtime or misses out on things they need.

- Portable, light, flexible, easy to use, a way to share ideas and learning.

- Organiser: music, phone, planner, storage device, voice recorder – means learning is organised, efficient and effective.

- Enhance learning through an online mentor, video conferencing.

- Facility to charge up portable devices.

- Back-up of devices needed.

- Variety of types of technology needs to be available (laptop, PDA, RM Asus miniBook, PC, Apple, etc.) – link the technology to learning style/preferences.

- Full compatibility with software.

- 1:1 ratio.

How wireless do we want to be?

- Anytime anywhere – with capacity to expand.

- Wi-Fi in social spaces.

- Instant access to data and systems.

- Some wireless-free zones needed.
- Server must be good enough.

What pieces of data would you need?

- Lesson plans, materials to be used for excluded students or staff support, homework, etc.
- Full student profile:
  - Medical details
  - Photograph
  - Attendance
  - Timetable
  - Intervention
  - Learning styles
  - Emotional/multiple intelligences
  - Preferred learning environment
  - Sensitive information
  - Performance against targets
  - Concerns
- List of absent staff and cover teachers.
- SLT availability.
- Important messages/announcements/reminders.
- Learning support strategies for generic and specific learning needs.

- School performance data – how do we compare locally/nationally?

What would IT support look like?

- Instant, planned, reliable, 'ICT rapid response unit'.

- Preventative maintenance, not just fixing.

- Human interaction – 'happy valued staff'.

- Staff empowerment/training needed at all levels.

- Request for support to be made through an instant communications system.

- Service level agreement (SLA) must cover all kit malfunctions.

How do we use Apple and Microsoft?

- 'The right tools for the job.'

- Facility for either dual boot or Apple iMac in specified areas (e.g. Art, Technology, Media).

- Student-friendly software – intuitive, tried and tested.

- Stay with the familiar, but enhance the Apple technology.

- Must be supported with training.

What would staff training look like?

- Should be for all learners: staff, parents, students and wider community.

- Training for the trainers to keep the expertise in school.

- Personalised and flexible – a combination of INSET, small groups, one-to-one, drop-in sessions, in planning, preparation and assessment time or twilight and evening.

- Facility for online tutorials and/or on CD.

- Accredited.

- Link training clearly with the kit and effective learning.

- Use as an opportunity to change teaching and learning styles.

- Training needed before the school is open.

What should an MLE/VLE do?

- Single sign-on.

- Secure.

- Instant data population.

- Access to range of teaching and learning resources:

  - Videoconferencing

  - Video demonstrations/revision sessions

  - Video record of work

  - Chatrooms to discuss lessons for limited periods

  - Message board

  - Home work

● Ability to communicate to a range of stakeholders, outside agencies (including Skype).

Some key quotations from the sessions:

'*We want to create a mobile theatre for learning*'

Member of staff

'*Children will not limit the use of technology – adults will*'

Parent

Appendix 4
CPD Learning Loop

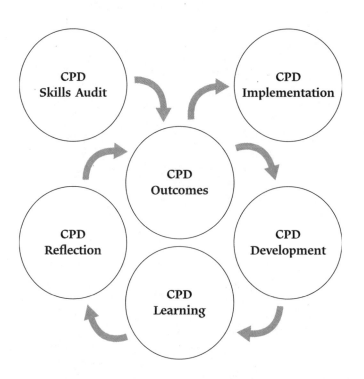

CPD Skills Audit

Derek filled in his questionnaire and had his one-to-one interview in which he expressed his fear of ICT, but recognised it could be a useful tool as long as he was not expected to use it all the time. Also wanted to develop groupwork skills to give it more rigour as worried students were opting out. Two CPD outcomes agreed: (a) to develop use of new equipment into lessons for 'awe and wonder' moments and (b) to implement a groupwork framework of rules.

CPD Outcomes

The published plan had several sessions which were of interest to Derek. Derek was assigned to two sessions but also opted for a third session. He was able to do this as sessions were repeated at different times to facilitate maximum engagement. Other colleagues did swaps within the faculty to maximise attendance and develop as wide and deep a skill base as possible.

CPD Development

Derek attended his session on the new IT equipment led by David Miller. It was his first time playing on the equipment and he was appreciative that the group size had been capped to enable him plenty of 'me time'! Derek suggested that he used images that students could annotate to show understanding. David added that Derek limit labels to the five most important to add challenge and promote independent thinking. The support plan was agreed: Derek would plan the lesson and have a play with HU5 with David, Jim Smith and Simon Britnell on standby.

CPD Learning

Derek planned the lesson in HU5 and colleagues joined him to see what was going on. All colleagues decided to use this lesson starter technique. Derek just checked with Jim about image resolution – a problem soon solved. Derek booked his class into HU5 and delivered the lesson.

CPD Reflection

Lesson went really well and the students enjoyed writing on the wall! Derek now wanted to know how to have different pen colours so that you could track different students' ideas. When Derek attended the next lesson with David this was soon cleared up. Derek had achieved his outcome and was now curious about some of the other sessions on offer.

CPD Implementation

This lesson technique was built into the new Scheme of Learning (SoL) for different topics and Derek had an item in the faculty meeting about how to use the technique. This meant that Shelia did not need to go to her session on this, instead opting for one on Excel.

Appendix 5

Curriculum Design: Our Starting Point (September 2008)

Priority 1

We want our learners to become independent enquirers and take responsibility for their own learning

By July 2010

Starting point – What are our learners like now?

Many of our learners focus on learning facts and being able to answer questions. In those subjects that encourage independent learning, our learners are curious and ask creative and reflective questions (about six out of ten roughly based on learning walks). This does not happen in all subject areas.

Coursework and the controlled assessment elements of GCSE and GCE qualifications are usually well presented but lack the depth and quality needed for higher marks.

Our learners are too reliant on teacher input (particularly at KS4) and find it hard to think of ways of tackling tasks set them.

41% of them made two levels of progress in English and 75% in Maths by the end of KS3. 65% gain the equivalent of 5A*–C GCSEs. Only 7.48% achieve A* and too high a proportion achieve D grades (13.9%).

At A level, the points per entry level has remained consistently good, but the points per student score could be higher – currently 672.67.

Design and implementation

Utilise £315,000 from BSF £2.1 million ICT budget to allow high quality bespoke training for staff to aid transition into new school and enhance learning.

Engage Independent Thinking (ITL) as the training provider to work with Mouchel to co-deliver explicit ICT training as well as pedagogical development. Insist on this being part of the ICT competitive tender process.

Develop an interview schedule for all staff, teaching and support, to highlight individual needs as regards training.

Work with the local authority on the development of Critical Skills as a pedagogical approach which has an emphasis on knowledge, dispositions and skills in learning.

Develop a transition curriculum for Year 7 with help from Roy Leighton from ITL. This incorporates the key principals of Critical Skills.

Developing a two-year training programme with Tim Sully to work with a key group of people to develop Critical Skills in the school.

Review progress

The development of the training programme led to a smooth move into the school.

It was recognised by the school's re-endorsement in Investors in People report.

Staff evaluations of CPD show a positive response and direct application in their work.

Controlled assessments: we had real problems with accessing ICT coursework for Years 10 and 11 due to the new system – this increased staff stress and delayed feedback on work. We have seen a lower than expected achievement in coursework for current year 11 in ICT.

5A*–C predictions for summer 2010 – 86% – column D (top 25% of the country).

Recruitment to sixth form is currently 65%.

The number of external applicants to the sixth form has risen to ten.

Set clear goals – What will our learners be like when we have achieved our priorities?

The large majority of learners will be curious and successful. They will be self-motivated, ask questions, find creative solutions and be clear about what interests them. Not only will they be good at taking tests and passing exams, they will be able to develop lines of thinking and show high levels of critical analysis and deeper under-standing. The school's specialist status will support this mode of enquiry.

They will achieve higher marks in coursework, controlled assessment and independently generated projects. Marks for externally assessed elements and controlled assess-ment will be equally balanced.

Over half of our learners will make two clear levels of progression in each key stage. Over 80% of learners will gain the equivalent of 5+A*–C grade passes and those learners whose column D target is an A* will achieve these grades.

At A2 level, the QCA points per student score will increase overall to 10% over the figure calculated from DCSF chances tables or ALPS. The recruitment of stu-dents will increase to 55% of the cohort and then to 60% of the cohort. Admissions from other schools will increase to 5 students per year.

Priority 2

We want our learners to achieve their best through a curriculum that is appropriate to them, particularly at KS4 and KS5.

By July 2010

Starting point – What are our learners like now?

Two thirds of our learners engage productively with a curriculum that incorporates themed learning opportunities at KS3, collapsed days for Citizenship across the school, a strong work based learning programme at KS4, with four option choices and some early GCSE provision in our specialist subjects. Our learners are not achieving the targets they should at KS4 and our school CVA is currently 995. Our learners need to push themselves to achieve the higher grades. Our KS3 results have improved over the past three years, with the school achieving column B targets and in some cases column D (Maths level 7, 2007).

Internal suspension – 76 days

Fixed term exclusions – 123 days

Whole school detentions – 197

Truancy – 49 incidents

Our sixth form learners engage with the courses on offer, with the profile of learners changing with the introduction of Level 2 courses such as public services. Our recruitment into the sixth form is of concern, as is the retention of students between Years 12 and 13. Our learners look elsewhere for course provision (Weston College).

Design and implementation

Develop the Creative and Media Diploma Line – organise training

Enhance delivery of BTECS.

Make ICT more accessible to students through BSF project – utilise it to engage learners and improve behaviour.

Train staff in the effective use of ICT in a range of areas through Mouchel/ITL trainers.

Review progress

Courses: 94% achieved three or four of their option choices at KS4. There are four BTEC courses along with Level 1 courses. A Diploma line was all set to run, but start-up funding was withdrawn.

Critical Skills is developed within the Year 7 transition curriculum and has received very positive feedback in our basic skills award, Quality Mark, as well as from pupils.

ICT is being used more extensively; laptop trolleys are in heavy use which allow flexibility in learning, especially in the use of break-out spaces.

Boys' engagement enhanced.

eBeam technology is patchy in use, with some SMART Board software being used.

800 computers to 1,200 students (approx.): 1:1.5/2 students.

CVA measure is 1,009, which is in the 'average' group of schools locally although considerably improved from 995.

Level 2 courses – public services ran in 2009, but unfortunately, there was not enough take-up for 2010 – something to be reviewed for September 2011.

Attendance has been hard to measure at first due to the technology – staff were not entering the marks into lesson monitor quickly enough, or completely forgetting.

Support staff struggled with some software that did not run on Citrix.

E-mail addresses a problem.

Attendance roughly 94%.

Fixed term exclusions October 2008 – ten students

October 2009 – one student (10% of previous year).

Set clear goals – What will our learners be like when we have achieved our priorities?

The large majority of our learners (85% and above) will be actively engaged in a course or topic of study that is appropriate to their future needs and aspirations. It will also be appropriate to their learning style, as well as offering pathways of progression from one key stage to another.

All our learners will use the specialist status of the school to enhance their learning through the use of ICT, media and technological resources and curriculum design (to be mapped across the curriculum in 2010).

Learners' attendance will be high (over 95%) and their behaviour exemplary (reduced internal suspensions, fixed term exclusions, detentions and truancy).

Over half of our learners will make two clear levels of progression in each key stage. Over 80% of learners will gain the equivalent of 5+A*-C grade passes and those learners whose column D target is an A* will achieve these grades. Our KS2-4 CVA measure will be within the 'above average' group of schools locally.

At A2 level, the QCA points per student score will increase overall to 10% over the figure calculated from DCSF chances tables or ALPS. The recruitment of students will increase to 55% of the cohort and then to 60% of the cohort. Admissions from other schools will increase to five students per year.

Priority 3

We want our learners to make informed choices about their learning pathways with access to a wide range of information advice and guidance.

By July 2010

Starting point – What are our learners like now?

Our learners make choices in their learning through course provision at KS3 (in Technology) as well as in the themed learning experiences, and through KS4 options, and KS5 sixth form application.

Not all students get the course of their choice at KS4 and while the curriculum we have is seen as 'good', our lower attaining learners do not have as high a range of options as other groups in the school.

Learners do not have to take a Technology or MFL subject at KS4.

Learners take part in mentoring sessions two to three times a year, with guidance towards targets given.

Discrete careers advice is given to our learners through a dedicated member of support staff in the careers base, as well as the Connexions service. Plan IT is used by our learners in Year 9 and Year 12. Our Year 8 and Year 9 learners do not currently receive discrete Information and Guidance (IAG), but experience work related learning during citizenship days.

Design and implementation

Develop the curriculum to provide a broad choice for students.

Transition curriculum to make learning 'real'.

Review progress

One permanent exclusion in 2009–10.

Five applications for early college transfer 2009–10.

Two students at KS4 educated off-site so not all learners engaged.

All students receive three reports a year with current level of attainment and key stage target.

All students receive academic monitoring with their tutor – KS4 students receive interviews with a representative from Connexions.

There is more to be done in IAG in Years 7, 8 and 9.

Summer 2009 – 5A*-C achievement was 75% (column D), 2010 predictions is currently 86% 5A*-C which is above the column D target of 81%

16+ predictions for summer 2010:

Target 25%, predicted 32% = +7%

B+ Target 50%, predicted 65% = +15%

C+ Target 75%, predicted 88% = +13%

Set clear goals – What will our learners be like when we have achieved our priorities?

All learners will be confident in the choices they make regarding the curriculum and pathways of progression. Our learners will understand why they need the skills/knowledge/understanding/qualification they are engaged in, and can see the purpose of their learning.

100% of students will achieve three or four first choice options at KS4 and these will offer equal opportunities to the learning needs of the students by gender, interest, ability and learning style.

All students will know their current level of attainment and key stage target, as well as strategies for improvement. Through mentoring, every learner will be known, valued and understood, with a clear pathway for success discussed with a lead professional.

The large majority of learners (75%+) will form positive, purposeful relationships within the classroom, and commitment to learning will be visible in the work completed, and learning outcomes achieved.

Targets for GCSE and 16+ achieved from column D FFT by 2010.

Appendix 6
'What If ...?' by Ian Gilbert

What if we are wrong?

What if we are all wrong?

What if the system in which we all work is not the best one for bringing the best out of young people?

What if, for some young people at least, it is the worst possible system?

What if we are doing more harm than good to young people by putting them through a system that is not suitable for their specific needs?

What if, when we say that a young person leaves school with nothing, we were to realise that what they leave with may be far worse than nothing? That leaving school with nothing would be letting us off lightly?

What if poor teachers aren't just bad at their job but actually doing harm? Not just ineffectual but destructive?

What if poor teaching were a crime?

What if allowing poor teaching in a school of which you were the head were more of a crime?

What if not knowing that the teaching was poor was more culpable than knowingly allowing it?

What if you were to ask of an interviewee, 'Do you love children?' Not simply teaching them, working with them, bringing the best out of them in a do-good social conscience sort of way but actually valuing them for who and what they are?

What if more secondary teachers realised that, first and foremost, they were there to teach children not subjects?

What if secondary schools were like primary schools?

What if dividing the world into compact boxes labelled, for example, history or art was the least effective way of seeing the world anyway?

What if the education system we have, which is the result of the application to education of industrialisation processes, has run its course and should go the way of the cotton mill or the coalmine?

What if forcing children to live with punishment or the threat of punishment wasn't the best way of forcing them to behave?

What if the behaviour we are forcing them to adopt isn't the behaviour that best serves them or the future anyway, that what we are experiencing in school is not poor behaviour but a wider social change in behaviours?

What if the things we teach young people are not the things they need to learn?

What if maths is not as important as, say, art or music?

What if many people were to admit that if they had spent more time as a child learning to play the piano and less time learning algebra they would probably be spending more time as an adult playing the piano than they do using algebra?

What if the qualifications with which children leave school don't actually count for very much beyond the world of education?

What if they count for nothing?

What if the skills developed in order to achieve those qualifications weren't actually to count for anything in later life?

What if those skills – writing neatly, spelling properly, sitting still, listening to instructions, doing as told, not questioning authority, being spoon fed – actually mitigated against success beyond school?

What if we were to take on board the neurological fact that a brain is not fully mature until it is 20 to 25 years old? And that boys' and girls' brains mature in different ways at different times? And that there may be a two to three year spread in the different levels of neurological maturation between children of the same age?

What if we asked where it was written that all 16 year olds are ready sit their exams on exactly the same day?

What if exams were actually one of the worst possible methods for assessing what a young person is capable of achieving?

What if, neurologically and psychologically, assessing people at 16 was the worst possible time to put a young person through such an ordeal?

What if the system was actually set up in order to sift one sort of person from another, as a social filter, yet that filter was now hopelessly out of date?

What if the highflying A-star students were the ones who were served most badly by schools?

What if sending a child out into the world with a string of academic successes but no experience of dealing with failure was the worst we could do to that child?

What if the children leaving school with the most qualifications were the ones least suitable for success in the working world beyond school? And the ones with the least the most?

What if employers refused to recognise qualifications as a way of identifying suitable employees and chose instead, say, hair colour or number of vowels in their first name?

What if the issue is not the underachievement of boys but the overachievement of girls?

What if we are teaching girls that working hard and writing neatly is the key to success when it isn't?

What if it is the key to serious mental harm in the long run?

What if the teaching unions were acting to hold back progress in education?

What if a combination of teaching young people how to learn, offering them things to learn that were relevant to them and to twenty-first century society and combining that with the most effective use of the most up-to-date technology meant that more young people would benefit more with fewer teachers?

What if the democratisation of knowledge meant the need for fewer subject specialists? That a caring generalist was better for the child than an uncaring specialist?

What if not allowing children to learn in a way that suits them best were a crime?

What if an adult were to accuse you, as the head teacher, of criminal neglect of your duty because your staff did not allow him to learn with something so simple as mind maps?

What if the system took into account the fact that the IQ model of assessing intelligence which makes some people clever and some just, say, good with their hands is an outdated model based on spurious research used in a misguided way for inappropriate reasons?

What if teachers worked on the premise that we all have perfect memories and that students forgetting what we have taught them is not a reflection on their ability or even our teaching but on the fact that we have not taken the time to show them how to use the memories they have?

What if children were not only aware of their own learning styles and preferences but also were to insist that their teachers helped them to learn accordingly at least for part of each lesson?

What if you were to take a willing but failing student from a lower ability group and work with that student one to one, offering him or her whatever help and support they needed to achieve from your best teachers?

What if then that student achieved a better GCSE grade than he or she would have done otherwise?

What if this served to prove that the system as it stands is desperately unsuitable for that student and thousands like them?

What if we acknowledged the irony of the fact that throughout their school career the child has to share the book, share the desk, share the equipment, share the computer, even share the teacher and then, right at the last minute, we throw them into an exam hall and tell them they are on their own? That we deny them one-to-one teaching but examine them in a one-to-one fashion?

What if we looked at a school that scored, say, 65% A–Cs at GCSE and asked if it felt happy that over a third of all its students had failed by the measure of success that has been set for them?

What if we asked if that was an effective use of the time, effort, energy and public money – that over a third of all of it was wasted?

What if it wasn't just wasted but actually served to do harm to a young person?

What if we saw, based on a national average of A–Cs at GCSE of just over 50%, that millions of pounds, millions of hours and thousands of adult lives had been spent in doing psychological harm to just under half the children in the country?

What if a school were to hear itself saying not 'We have a target this year of 55% A–Cs' but 'We are aiming to ensure that 45% of our students will fail this year'?

What if a school were to set a goal of 100% A–Cs, whatever the cost, not in money, but to the system?

What if, after repeatedly telling young people to think for themselves, they actually did?

What if they thought for themselves that the system was not appropriate for them and refused to play along with it any more, not in a belligerent or aggressive way but just by saying no?

What if all the students who were taught by incompetent teachers simply refused to go to that teacher's lesson?

What if they all just went to a good teacher's lesson instead? What if every student in your school refused to go through the exam process believing it to be flawed?

What if all the teachers in the country were to say no – not in the form of any misguided industrial procedure but simply to highlight the fact that if the job involves working so hard so often then the processes behind the job must be wrong?

What if teaching something in which we don't believe, in a system we feel may be fundamentally flawed, means we are actually teaching young people that beliefs, honesty and integrity are not relevant in adult life?

What if the union rep who told me recently that the majority of teachers, were they to have their time again, would not go back into teaching was right?

What if not enjoying our job is sending the message to young people that jobs are not to be enjoyed?

What if we were to ask ourselves about the specific purpose of the education system and whether that was different from the specific purpose of education?

What if the two were incompatible? That serving the specific needs of the system meant that we ended up neglecting the specific needs of the child?

What if we asked, once we had identified the purpose of education, if we were achieving that goal for all of our students?

What if we put self-esteem – feeling capable and loveable – as our number one goal, more important than qualifications?

What if we were to identify the purpose of a life and then seek to equip young people with the skills necessary to achieve it?

What if we were to treat teaching not as a job but as the work of gods, whose every word and deed had some subsequent consequence that resonated for all time?

What if more of us acted strongly on what we felt most strongly about?

What if you were to put this article down now and go for a walk?

First published by the Association of School and College Learners in 2004

Bibliography

Association of School and College Leavers (2010). *The Impact of a Changing Economy*. 2020 Future: Briefing Paper 8. Leicester: ASCL.

BBC News (2005). Head teacher stress is 'rising'. Available at www.http://news.bbc.co.uk/1/hi/education/4447232.stm> accessed 20 May 2011.

Bowkett, S., Harding, T., Lee, T. and Leighton, R. (2008). *Happy Families*. London: Network Continuum.

Bristow, M., Ireson, G. and Coleman, A. (2007). *A Life in the Day of a Headteacher: A Study of Practice and Well-Being*. Nottingham: National College for School Leadership.

Covey, S. R. (1999). *Principle-Centred Leadership*. New York: Simon & Schuster.

Cowan, C. and Beck, D. (1996). *Spiral Dynamics: Mastering Values, Leadership, and Change*. Oxford: Blackwell.

Curran, A. (2008). *The Little Book of Big Stuff About the Brain*. Carmarthen: Crown House Publishing.

Department for Children, Schools and Families (2010). *Third Annual Report of the Price Waterhouse Coopers Evaluation of Building Schools for the Future*. London: DCSF.

Department for Education and Skills and Commission for Architecture and the Built Environment (2005). *Picturing School Design*. London: DfES and CABE.

Education by Design (1997), *Level 1 Coaching Kit*. Gosport: Hants: Education by Design.

Eley, J. (2003). *Creating Excellent Buildings: A Guide for Clients*. London: CABE.

Friedman, T. L. (2005). *The World is Flat*. London: Penguin.

Fullan, M. (2001). *Leading in a Culture of Change*. San Francisco, CA: Jossey-Bass.

Gilbert, I. (2004a). *Little Owl's Book of Thinking*. Carmarthen: Crown House Publishing.

Gilbert, I. (2004b). What If ...? Leicester: Association of School and College Leaders. Available at www.independentthinking.co.uk/Cool+Stuff/Articles/108.aspx, accessed 20 May 2011.

Kelly, G. and New, D. (2009). *So, You Want To Build a New School? Available at* www.independentthinking.co.uk/Cool+stuff/handouts/661.aspx> accessed 5 July 2011.

Lucas, B., Claxton, G. and Webster, R. (2010). *Mind the Gap: Research and Reality in Practical and Vocational Education*. London: Edge Foundation/Centre for Real World Learning.

Puttnam, D. and Barber, M. (2009). *We Are the People We've Been Waiting For*. Documentary film. New Moon Television.

Richardson, T. (2005). *Assessment at Key Stages One and Two: Evaluation of the Effectiveness of Teacher Assessments.* Bristol: Serco Learning Consultancy.

Rogers, C. and Freiberg, H. J. (1983). *Freedom to Learn.* London: Prentice Hall.

Ryan, W. (2008). *Leadership with a Moral Purpose.* Carmarthen: Crown House Publishing.

Tan, H. C., Anumba, C. J., Carrillo, P. M., Bouchlaghem, D., Kamara, J. and Udeaja, C. (2010). *Capture and Reuse of Project Knowledge in Construction.* Oxford: Wiley-Blackwell.

Weatherley, C. (2000). *Leading the Learning School.* Stafford: Network Educational Press.

Wragg, T., Wragg, C. and Chamberlin, R. (2004). *Jersey Critical Skills Programme: An Evaluation.* Jersey: Department for Education, Sport and Culture.

Praise for *Where will I do my pineapples?*

Having been involved in BSF at a Local Authority level for the past five years, this was the book people had been asking for all along. "Can you put us in touch with someone who has done this already?" Being in wave one, the answer was, for most of the time, "Er ... no."

So, I very much looked forward to reading this book.

It is an interesting, reassuring and useful read and it's clear from the way it is written that to enter the process without taking your sense of humour along for the ride is an unwise move. In fact, a sense of humour and an acceptance of the ridiculous is essential!

So much did the accurate description of the BSF process resonate, that at times I could feel my blood pressure rising in a way that only those who have experienced the endless rounds of meetings, BSF lingo and frustrations with bureaucracy can appreciate.

For those of us who have experienced BSF, it was reassuring that we were not alone, and it was a prompt for reflection. For those still to go through the process, it will be a very useful guide to how it feels from an SLT point of view, with valuable reminders that the people involved are the key to the success of the project. (N.B. Although the BSF process has been halted in its tracks by many authorities - the chances are that you will at some point experience a new build and, in any case, the contents of this book ring true for any change process.)

The book is a good balance of education and management theory, supported and illustrated by anecdotes, examples and soul-searching.

The Do's and Don'ts section at the end of each chapter is a particularly useful quick reference for any leaders of any change project, and are unashamedly focused on making sure that everyone is involved and cared for. Although one tends to learn most from one's own mistakes, to ignore the experiences and lessons learned in this book, could seem reckless.

Yvonne Lewington, Education Consultant
(From Good to Outstanding)

This is a book about wisdom and integrity: having the wisdom to make judgements about what other people say, and the integrity to stick to sound educational principles. It asks what learning is all about, and comes up with some practical answers that are of interest even if you do not have the blessing (or curse) of a new school building to plan. It looks at how best to organise people and spaces within a learning community and is honest about pitfalls and partial successes. It gives great advice about how to deal with resistance from staff which will be of use to anyone in the business of trying to herd cats (or school management as it is otherwise known). It is also about creating a vision and then clinging to it no matter what happens.

I would recommend this book to anyone in school management, not just those involved in building a new school site. The nuggets of wisdom in the appendix are almost worth buying the book for on their own.

Jane Werry, Director of Music & Lead Teacher, Hayes School

This account of how one school used the opportunity of a rebuilding programme to rethink its educational philosophy will be of interest beyond a professional readership.

Emphasising the fundamental importance of putting learning and the learner at the heart of planning it gives a clear, practical and frank account of a sometimes fraught process.

Drawing on pedagogical and psychological research it contains lessons about the nature of leadership and the role of technology as well as the state of education.

Each chapter concludes with a useful list of Dos and Don'ts` for anyone finding themselves in the same position as the author.

Richard Yelland, OECD Directorate for Education

A new building is a lot more than bricks, paint and glass. In the case of Nailsea school, their BSF project presented the opportunity to challenge `traditional methods of schooling and build a learning community based on a clear vision of what was best for the learners passing through the new doors.

This book shows us the importance of vision, bravery and the human touch in making lasting sustainable change to the way a school is run. Gill Kelly's unswerving commitment to providing the best possible learning environment shaped every decision made in the project, from the ICT provision to the design of the curriculum. Project managing a multi million pound build whilst teaching and managing a school provides its own unique challenges, but this book tackles the issues of inexperience, overload and self-doubt candidly and with tips gleaned from the journey.

At its heart, this is a book about people: how to help them deal with the scary prospect of a new way of working in an unfamiliar space; how to support and encourage them whilst challenging expectations of what learning should look and feel like; how to keep your own sanity when the job is all-consuming and never-ending and everything is a priority; how to build and maintain successful teams, both at leadership level and in the learning environment. Once again, the concepts of belief in the vision, bravery and communication are paramount. It shows what is possible when professional educators do not allow themselves to be swayed by the vagaries of government, outside agencies or suppliers and believe in themselves as experts in their field.

Andy Colley, Advanced Skills Teacher.

More Little Books ...

The Little Book of Thunks®: 260 questions to make your brain go ouch! by Ian Gilbert ISBN: 9781845900625

The Little Book of Big Stuff About the Brain: The True Story of Your Amazing Brain by Andrew Curran edited by Ian Gilbert ISBN: 9781845900854

The Little Book of Music for the Classroom: Using Music to Improve Memory, Motivation, Learning and Creativity by Nina Jackson edited by Ian Gilbert ISBN: 9781845900915

The Little Book of Inspirational Teaching Activities: Bringing NLP into the Classroom by David Hodgson edited by Ian Gilbert ISBN: 9781845901363

The Little Book of Values: Educating Children to Become Thinking, Responsible and Caring Citizens by Julie Duckworth edited by Ian Gilbert ISBN: 9781845901356

The Little Book of Charisma: Applying the Art and Science by David Hodgson edited by Ian Gilbert ISBN: 9781845902933

The Little Book of Bereavement for Schools by Ian Gilbert with William, Olivia and Phoebe Gilbert ISBN: 9781845904647

Little Owl's Book of Thinking: An Introduction to Thinking Skills by Ian Gilbert ISBN: 9781904424352

Dancing About Architecture: A Little Book of Creativity by Phil Beadle edited by Ian Gilbert ISBN: 9781845907259

The Perfect (Ofsted) Lesson by Jackie Beere edited by Ian Gilbert ISBN: 978-184590460-9

The Book of Thunks®: Is not going fishing a hobby? and other possibly impossible questions to stretch your brain and annoy your friends by Ian Gilbert ISBN: 9781845900922